I0819617

SMALL TOWNS U.S.A.

The town square in Healdsburg, California (page 316), is central to many boutiques, restaurants, and wineries.

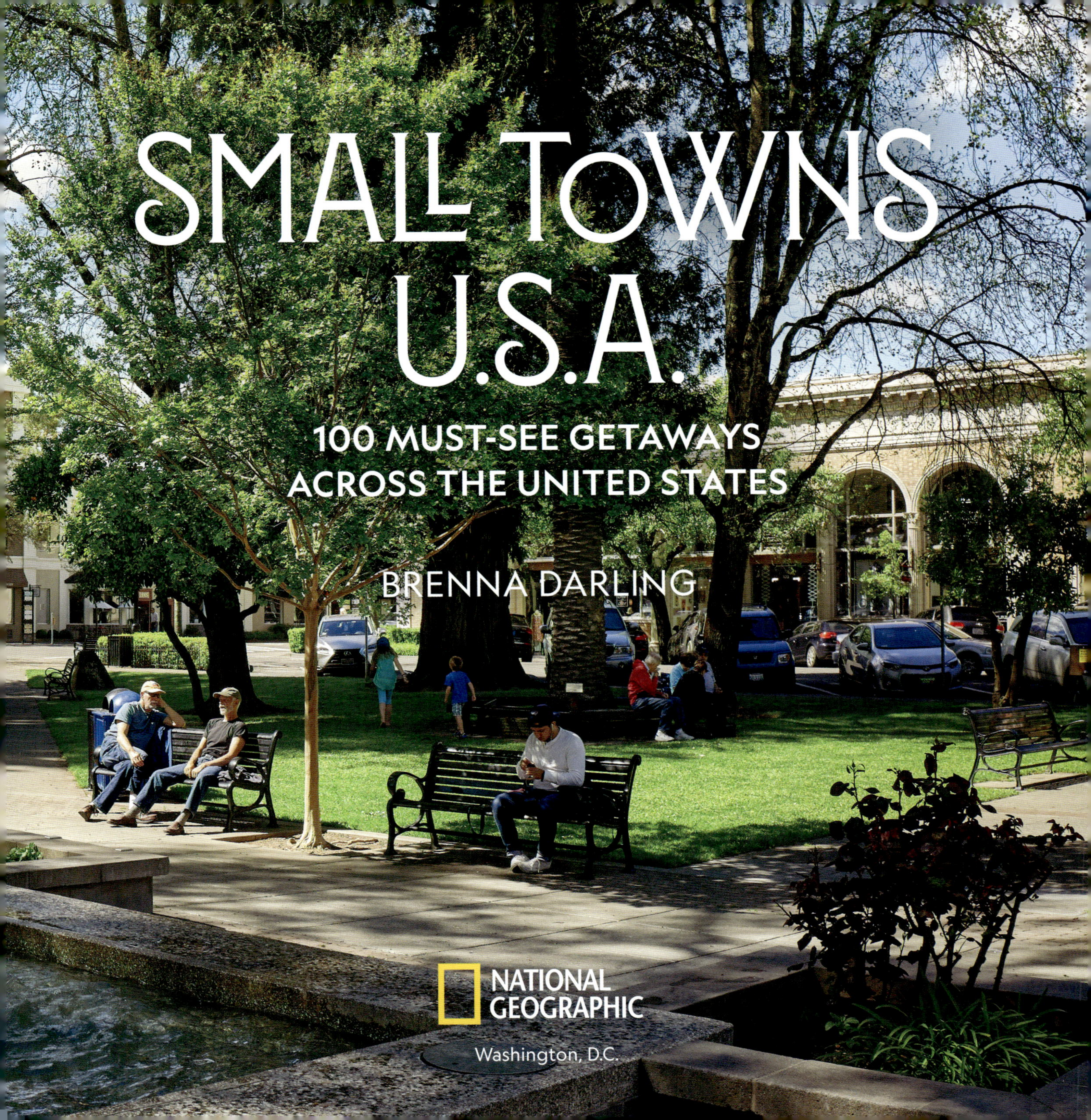

SMALL TOWNS U.S.A.

100 MUST-SEE GETAWAYS ACROSS THE UNITED STATES

BRENNA DARLING

NATIONAL GEOGRAPHIC

Washington, D.C.

CONTENTS

A pink and purple sunset washes over the docks of Portsmouth, New Hampshire (page 56).

BEGIN

INTRODUCTION

There's something nostalgic about a road trip to a small town for a weekend getaway. My childhood in Colorado was sprinkled with memories of hopping in the van and exploring mountain towns nearby. In the summer, it was driving across sunny mountain passes from Ouray to Telluride; in the winter, it was snowshoeing amid the evergreen trees in Estes Park. For my family, it was a way to spend time together that felt exciting, while also being accessible and budget friendly. That joy of exploration stuck with me as I grew up and moved to Los Angeles—admittedly the opposite of a small place! My boyfriend (now husband) Humberto and I would sneak out of the city for long weekends away, more often than not finding ourselves in small towns up and down the coast: Paso Robles for wine tasting and brewery tours, Solvang for horseback riding and *kringle* sampling. Whether it was the local charm or the slower pace of life, I always found that I could breathe deeper and truly unwind while visiting small towns in America.

Then, amid the world-altering COVID-19 pandemic in 2020, I took stock of my life. After being stuck at home for months, I was gripped by an urge to explore the small towns in states farther afield. So with Humberto and my dog, Walker, along for the ride, I set out on a road trip to find the greatest small towns I'd never heard of. From their big-time community spirit to adventurous outdoor opportunities, I gained new appreciation for those off-the-beaten-path destinations. Along the way, I realized that the important things in life can be found in small places.

That one decision changed the trajectory of my life. We decided to leave our home in LA and settle down in Colorado. And we kept taking regular road trips to continue exploring. Ultimately those explorations led to the book you hold in your hands.

Five hundred eucalyptus trees form a famed tree tunnel over Maluhia Road, the gateway to Kōloa, Hawaii (page 340).

HOTEL
PARKING
PARKING
PARKING
PARKING

OYSTER BAY
RESTAURANT
GAMING
CALAMITY'S
HISTORIC
CLUB
HISTORIC SITE
SALOON NUMBER 10
WHERE
WILD BILL WAS SHOT
AUGUST 2 1876
DEADWOOD
WILD BILL
BAR
STOP

It turns out, the United States is a "nation of small towns," as the U.S. Census Bureau put it in a 2020 article. Of the 19,500 incorporated places (designated towns and cities), nearly 75 percent have populations under 5,000. So how did I narrow this collection down to just 100? First, I had to define what I mean by "small town." For the parameters of this book, I determined that the towns had to be small relative in size to the state they are located in. For example, in a state like California, with a population of 39 million, and with a couple of cities that surpass one million residents, I could comfortably label a town as "small" if it had 40,000 or fewer residents. In a state like Vermont, with a total population of about 624,000, I chose towns that had under 10,000 residents.

I wanted at least one town represented in all 50 states, and each town needed to stand on its own as a destination, with bucolic landscapes and plenty of fun things to do. A great town needs to honor historic sites and buildings or use them wisely for new, more modern purposes. This is what I like to call "historic flair." Next, there must be places of interest for visitors, whether it's museums, distinguishing landmarks, or food and drink options that show off the flavor of the town. Outdoor activity options, either directly in the town or just outside it, are also essential to give visitors a real sense of adventure. I favored towns with a Main Street that incorporates art—in a real way, with a sense of community—through local stores, coffeehouses, galleries, or murals. Boutique lodging—thoughtful, town-specific accommodations that exude a sense of welcome in a way that generic chain hotels or motels often do not—was a must to keep a town in the running. I also paid attention to the festivals, annual events, and traditions that were a point of town pride. Finally, restaurants and brewery or winery options sealed the deal, giving these special places that "I can't wait to go back there" type of vibe for visitors.

When I asked residents what their favorite part about living in their town was, the overwhelming response was the sense of community. I heard this again and again, from the Pacific Northwest to the Deep South and from people of all walks of life. While each town is special in its own right, their individual communities desire what we all want in life: Moments to create memories with loved ones. A place to put up your feet and enjoy the view. Opportunity for adventure, followed by a tasty meal. It is my belief that our core human desires remain the same. My travels to small-town America have proved this to be true.

My hope is that this book inspires you to explore the country with fresh eyes. There is a small town for everyone. Return to this book for a weekend getaway, a family vacation, a trip with friends, a road trip. Hopefully I'll see you on Main Street.

LEFT: The annual Cane River Zydeco Festival brings music, dancing, and fun to Natchitoches, Louisiana (page 144), every Labor Day weekend. PAGES 8-9: The supposedly haunted Fairmont Hotel in Deadwood, South Dakota (page 282), immerses visitors in the spirit of the Old West. The hotel is home to the Oyster Bay Bar & Casino.

PART ONE
NORTHEAST

Rolling hills and grazing cows mark the scenic drives around Woodstock, Vermont (page 98).

BULLS BRIDGE
KENT, CONNECTICUT

KENT

CONNECTICUT

A scenic two-hour drive from New York City takes you to the quaint town of Kent, Connecticut. Known for its vibrant arts scene, covered bridges, and waterfalls, Kent blends old and new in a way that makes it a charming weekend destination. So charming, in fact, that every October, it hosts the Firelight Event (formerly Fan Fest), during which it assumes the guise of the fictional television town of Stars Hollow during a three-day *Gilmore Girls* celebration.

The arts elevate Kent's refined atmosphere. Metal sculptures by artists Joy Brown and Peter Busby dot the landscape around town. The Kent Barns—a collection of restored barns used for shops, art galleries, and eateries—adjacent to Main and Maple Streets, is a favorite spot to dine, offering delicious wood-fired pizzas and a seasonal menu. Before or after dinner, take a short drive east to Kent Falls Brewing Company, which has a taproom set in a red barn on a working farm. The beers have witty names like Awkward Hug and Haircuts for Everybody.

While in town, stop at Bulls Bridge, originally built in 1760 and reconstructed in 1842. Spanning the Housatonic River, it stands as one of the few covered bridges in Connecticut. Legend states that George Washington crossed Bulls Bridge during the Revolutionary War—visit to walk in his footsteps. Afterward, head to Kent Falls State Park or Macedonia Brook State Park for hiking. Kent Falls features the eponymous 250-foot tiered waterfall, and Macedonia Brook offers views of both the Catskill and Taconic Mountains.

Take a stroll across 109-foot-long Bulls Bridge, added to the National Register of Historic Places in 1972.

TALK LIKE A LOCAL

"GRINDER"

It's lunchtime and you're looking for a sandwich. When in Connecticut, order a grinder. These sandwiches—called subs in other parts of the country—have hot fillings nestled inside a roll of thick Italian bread. The hearty bread may point to the origins of the name: The durable Italian loaves require extra chewing, or "grinding."

MYSTIC

CONNECTICUT

The charming seaside town of Mystic is one of the most popular summer retreats in Connecticut, and it's easy to see why. While the population of Mystic hovers around 5,000 permanent residents, it offers big-city amenities with small-town charm. Influenced by the rich history of whaling, boatmaking, and clamming, Mystic offers award-winning restaurants, beautiful ocean views, and plenty to do for the whole family.

Before you hit the water, visit the Mystic Seaport Museum, an interactive village spread out on a few acres along the Mystic River. Over time, historic 19th-century buildings around Connecticut were saved, moved to the museum, and restored to re-create a slice of past New England coastal life. It's easy to spend an entire day here. Docents throughout demonstrate how to make traditional roasted oysters, operate a printing press, and tie sailing knots. America's only remaining original whaling boat is docked here and available to tour, too. Weekend festivals and events, like the popular Mystic Folkways Music Festival and the Community Carol Sing, are typically held by the museum in wintertime. Stop by the museum's Schaefer's Spouter Tavern for lobster rolls and a Dark 'n' Stormy (a cocktail of dark rum, ginger beer, and lime juice), which you can take to go while enjoying the rest of the museum property.

Mystic's downtown waterfront district is filled with colonial-era captains' homes and historic landmarks and is split in two by the Mystic River Bascule Bridge, a drawbridge that is the only way to get from one

The Thompson Exhibition Building, with its evocative curving roof, is the centerpiece of the Mystic Seaport Museum.

TASTE OF THE REGION

HOT LOBSTER ROLL

The hot lobster roll, a mix of buttered lobster claw and tail meat piled high on a toasted bun, is a Connecticut staple. The debate between which version of the lobster roll is better—the hot Connecticut style or the chilled, creamy Maine style—rages on between New Englanders, but either way, diners always come out on top.

Mystic's Sift Bake Shop offers French-focused goods including macarons, entremets, and sandwich cookies.

side of town to the other. You might have to stop to wait for a passing ship, but the maritime bustle is part of the charm. One of the most recognizable destinations on the waterfront is Mystic Pizza, a third-generation restaurant made famous by the eponymous 1988 film starring Julia Roberts. The pizza is delicious and worth the wait. Bank and Bridge Brewing—a veteran-owned brewery and kitchen housed in an old marble bank building—is next door. Main Street is home to enough dining options, pubs, and nautical shops to fill a lovely afternoon of exploring. One of note: Sift Bake Shop is an award-winning and nationally recognized French bakery and rooftop bar, ideal for enjoying croissants, macarons, and carrot cake roulade.

During warmer months, the Mystic River is busy with kayakers, paddleboarders, and guided cruises. Check out nearby Bluff Point State Park or Haley Farm State Park for hiking and biking trails. Colder months bring about annual festivals such as the Charity Chowder Cook Off and the Cabin Fever Festival, hosted at the Olde Mistick Village. This open-air village began welcoming visitors in 1973 and is the place to shop for Mystic-made souvenirs and artisanal gifts, and it's another option for excellent restaurants and bakeshops.

REHOBOTH BEACH

DELAWARE

The salty Atlantic air permeates the breeze, as waves crash on the pristine sandy shore. Peals of laughter and the slaps of flip-flops supply the background noise. A timber boardwalk stretches along the coastline between Rehoboth's beach and town, coming together to make the "nation's summer capital" in Delaware. Beachgoers from up and down the East Coast venture here to soak in the sun and enjoy the sand. The lively boardwalk is home to Funland, an iconic amusement park founded in 1961 with rides that rise high above the quaint skyline. Down the road, visitors will find Shell We Golf, a kitschy miniature golf course, and plenty more to do off the beach, including strolling a charming downtown.

There is no shortage of excellent places to grab a bite. The sand patio, palm fronds, and murals of Somewhere at the Beach make a cool environment to grab brunch or tacos, paired with tropical cocktails like the Reho Sour (a lime, lemon, and bourbon cocktail with a red-wine twist). For a casual fine-dining experience, check out the ocean-and-farm-to-table cuisine at Salt Air. The atmosphere feels comfortable yet special—it's a great date-night spot. For a sweet treat, fill up a bag of saltwater taffy from Dolles Candyland. The bright-orange "Dolles" sign has been a Delaware landmark since the candy shop opened on the boardwalk in 1926.

Rehoboth Beach bustles at the height of summer. You can rent umbrellas, chairs, and other beach equipment from local vendors.

ADVENTURE ALONG THE WAY

DEWEY BEACH

After a day in the sun at Rehoboth Beach, make the short drive to Dewey Beach for a night out on the mile-long town. The Bottle and Cork, one of Delaware's best music venues, holds concerts throughout the week with well-known performers along with a slew of cover bands. Its Saturday Jam is a raucous flagship event, drawing huge crowds (of mostly college students and young twentysomethings) from May through September. Live music floats from the weathered wooden decks of many other ocean-side restaurants in Dewey Beach, and the atmosphere is energetic and welcoming to all looking for a good time.

A free concert series takes place at the Rehoboth Beach Bandstand on summer weekends with performances by a range of local acts and tribute bands.

Festivals throughout the year draw huge crowds and instill a sense of town pride. The Sea Witch Festival in October is a family-friendly weekend of parades, costume contests, and monster-themed trick-or-treating. The Summer Concert Series brings in free performances each weekend at the open-air bandstand right off the beach.

Cape Henlopen State Park lies north of town and offers hiking and biking trails as well as opportunities to be on the water via kayaking, paddleboarding, clamming, or boating. The designated Point of Cape Henlopen is where the Atlantic Ocean meets the Delaware Bay. You can tour the Fort Miles Museum here to see an unusual World War II-era American defense site, constructed to take advantage of Delaware's strategic positioning. South of Rehoboth Beach, Delaware Seashore State Park is a beautiful coastal site to surf, fish, and enjoy pristine views of undeveloped coastline, salt marshes, and the Indian River Inlet Bridge.

TASTE OF THE REGION

SALTY FRENCH FRIES WITH VINEGAR

Thrasher's has been serving up thick-cut, salty french fries since it opened in 1929. A true Delawarean knows that malt vinegar is the secret weapon for making these the perfect beachside staple. Don't even ask for ketchup; they won't have it or recommend it.

TRT
TRIPLE RAIL TURN
TRT
TRIPLE RAIL TURN
TRT

BAR HARBOR

MAINE

Tucked along the rocky coastline of Frenchman Bay on Mount Desert Island, and considered the gateway to Acadia National Park (just three miles away), is the charming seaside town of Bar Harbor. Clapboard storefronts line Main Street, and colorful buoys are hooked along the building exteriors on the Town Pier. Natural beauty, maritime history, and New England charm coalesce to create a fantastic destination in the Pine Tree State.

Start your tour downtown at the Abbe Museum, a Smithsonian affiliate, to get a better understanding of the history and culture of the region's Indigenous people. For 12,000 years, the Wabanaki—specifically the Passamaquoddy and Penobscot tribes—used Mount Desert Island for hunting, trading, fishing, and clam digging. When painters in the 1850s shared the island's beauty through artworks of stunning mountain and seascapes, a wave of summer visitors, known as rusticators, flocked to Mount Desert Island.

Sunrise on Cadillac Mountain can look especially psychedelic because of the peak's trippy pink granite.

The wealthy elite built lavish cottages to rival those found in Newport, Rhode Island, and the subsequent Gilded Age cemented Bar Harbor as a vacationland.

In 1947, a devastating fire swept through the island, lasting 10 days and destroying 170 homes and five historic hotels in downtown Bar Harbor. It destroyed 67 seasonal estates on Millionaires' Row. The island rebounded, and you can still see many of those restored summer cottages in reenergized modern-day Bar Harbor.

TASTE OF THE REGION

BLUEBERRY PIE

Made with wild Maine blueberries (the official state fruit), blueberry pie is naturally the official state dessert. Maine's cold barrens introduce a slight acidity and hardiness to the native wild blueberries, and the fruit's mildly sweet flavor works perfectly in baked goods. Wild blueberries are chock-full of antioxidants and anti-inflammatory properties, so you can rightly consider blueberry pie a "healthy" choice.

Downtown Bar Harbor features art galleries and boutiques alongside specialty food stores, including seafood purveyors (with some offering take-home lobster bakes).

Today, the town and surrounding area offer no shortage of opportunities for epic outdoor excursions. The crags of Cadillac Mountain, one of the premier destinations in Acadia National Park, illuminate with a kaleidoscope of orange, pink, and purple as the first rays of the rising sun stretch across the sky. Sitting at 1,530 feet, the summit of Cadillac Mountain is the highest point on the East Coast shoreline. From fall to the spring solstice, it's the first piece of land to see the sun on the entire continental United States, so its trails are popular for early-rising hikers. Find another great hike on Acadia's Sand Beach: The Beehive, a giant granite rock face, has convenient metal handrails to help you up a steep 500-foot climb. You'll be rewarded with panoramic views of the bay. Sand Beach is also a great spot for a spectacular evening of stargazing; pack a picnic and head to this secluded cove, which is only accessible from a cliffside staircase and is protected from wind and surrounding light sources. Be careful swimming here—even in the summer the water temperatures are frigid, and there can also be strong tides.

For more seafaring folk, Egg Rock Light, built in 1875, is one of the region's most pristine historic lighthouses, and best seen by boat. Sea lions bask on the rocks, and common eiders, herring gulls, and double-crested cormorants swoop through the air. You can kayak, canoe, fish, or sail in Frenchman Bay. Charter a schooner for a lobster-picnic cruise and

THE STADIUM
THE STADIUM BAR HARBOR
Lobster Rolls
Bakery · Crepes
Popovers · Gifts
Coffee Hound
The STADIUM
BEN & BILL'S
CHOCOLATE EMPORIUM
CANDIES
COFFEE
ICE CREAM
MADE FRESH DAILY

OPPOSITE TOP: Lobster buoys appear in a variety of colors. **OPPOSITE BOTTOM:** Popovers are distinguished by their steep sides and fluffy tops. **LEFT:** Climb to the top of Acadia National Park's Beehive rock for views over Frenchman Bay.

look for porpoises, sharks, whales, and seals in the salty serene blue waters. At low tide, walk the land bridge to Bar Island to hunt for sea glass—just mind the tides so you can make it back across safely.

The best dining in Bar Harbor is local, fresh, and immersive. Within Acadia National Park, Jordan Pond House is famous for its buttery popovers, grassy lawn surrounded by pine and hemlock trees, and views of the eponymous pond. In town, the bait-to-plate model is king. Havana infuses Latin flavors with lobster and paella dishes. Project Social Kitchen and Bar serves up fresh oysters and scallops on a tree-covered patio. Crack into a kettle-steamed lobster with hot drawn butter on the pier at Stewman's. And during the epic peak foliage season, a Leaf-Peeping Ale from Atlantic Brewing Company hits the spot. Bar Harbor encourages visitors to shop local, eat local, and enjoy all Maine has to offer.

TALK LIKE A LOCAL

"THE BEANAH"

The classic American brand L. L. Bean was founded in Maine, with its famous flagship store in Freeport, where you'll find a larger-than-life "Bean Boot" at the front door. The brand has transcended retail clothing and outdoor gear and become, for many, a way of life, so much so that Mainers drop the "L. L." and simply call it "the Beanah" or "Beans."

CAMDEN

MAINE

The laid-back coastal town of Camden sits on Penobscot Bay in Maine's mid-coast region. Home to the only ocean-view ski area on the East Coast (the Camden Snow Bowl), it offers a wealth of outdoor opportunities paired with a historic opera house that hosts international performers and an annual film festival. Camden embodies the tranquil vacationland reputation of the state, and its population nearly triples during peak summer season.

Hike up Mount Battie in Camden Hills State Park for a phenomenal view of the town and a panorama of the entire bay. Sail Penobscot Bay from the deck of a chartered schooner and spot puffin colonies on the shorelines or gray seals swimming alongside the hull of your boat. Swim or kayak in the fresh waters of Barrett's Cove at the spring-fed Megunticook Lake.

After adventuring, enjoy the catch of the day at a number of restaurants. For a true Maine experience, drive the winding coastal roads to McLoons Lobster Shack for a buttery lobster roll. On Main Street, Sea Dog Brewing Company serves up award-winning beers, including its beloved Blueberry Wheat Ale. Owl and Turtle Bookshop Café is a great spot to grab a coffee and browse for new books before heading out on the day's excursions. Stay at Whitehall, just a 10-minute walk from downtown. The gorgeous inn has bay views and cozy outdoor firepits that encourage guests to unwind under the stars.

Mount Battie is a terrific viewpoint for a fireworks show over Camden Harbor.

TASTE OF THE REGION

EAST COAST OYSTERS

The briny flavor of East Coast oysters makes them distinct from oysters found in other parts of the country. East Coast oysters are served chilled, typically on a bed of ice, with a little cocktail or mignonette sauce and a squeeze of fresh lemon juice—all you have to do is slurp and enjoy. Follow the Maine Oyster Trail—an online guide to the top oyster spots in the state—for the ultimate seafood lovers' adventure.

NUTCRACKER MAGIC

BERLIN

MARYLAND

The beginning of June can only mean one thing in Berlin: the highly anticipated annual Bathtub Races. The streets shut down and carts made from modified bathtubs whiz down the road in a competition for bragging rights and the coveted glass rubber-ducky trophy. The town's chamber of commerce hosts the event, local news stations broadcast it, and onlookers cheer on their favorite competitors from the sidewalks. It's a signature of a town that is known to be one of the coolest in the country.

Located about 10 miles from the Atlantic coastline, Berlin is filled with history and charm. The quirky, vibrant tree-lined Main Street was revitalized by a joint effort between citizens, businesses, and the town government beginning in the late 1980s. Many of its Victorian buildings are listed on the National Register of Historic Places. And there's a delightful dichotomy between the preserved past and the artistic present, with colorful awnings adorning many shop facades. A sense of community and town pride can be felt everywhere you turn.

Main Street and a few offshoot streets make a highly walkable and shoppable downtown, with more than 60 boutiques. Check out Honey Water for candles made in collaboration with local farms, or pick up fresh blooms at the flower bar at Eastern Woodland Home. The Globe, a former theater turned cocktail bar and lounge, is the place to be for Martini Mondays and Karaoke Thursdays. Rustic

Eastern Woodland Home on Pitt Street sells a variety of charming houseplants and vintage goods.

TALK LIKE A LOCAL

"DMV"

Anywhere else in the country, the DMV is where you go to renew your driver's license, but Marylanders who live close to the nation's capital use "DMV" as a catchall term to refer to the District of Columbia and the surrounding counties in Maryland and Virginia. Luckily, Maryland doesn't have a Department of Motor Vehicles—it's instead called the MVA (Motor Vehicle Administration). That should clear up any confusion.

Since 1990, Berlin's Main Street has played host to the Bathtub Races, during which racers in homemade carts compete in front of a cheering crowd of onlookers.

Burley Oak Brewing Company, just off Main Street, incorporates a coastal edge in some of its brews (try the Sea Heathen pilsner). Rom-com fans can look for locales from the fictional town of Hale in Julia Roberts's 1998 film *Runaway Bride,* which was filmed in Berlin.

Main Street sits on land that was once a thoroughfare for the local Assateague people and the bordering Pocomoke tribe. During colonial times, the region was used as part of the Burley Plantation. Berlin most likely got its name from a contraction of the name Burleigh Inn, which was a popular tavern at the bustling intersection between the Philadelphia Post and Sinepuxent Roads in the 1700s. Several homes from this era are available for tours, such as the 1740-era Rackliffe House and the federal-style Taylor House Museum, originally built in 1832. The Inn Berlin is housed in a lovely blue Victorian on a grassy grand estate with twinkly café lights strung between trees in the garden. Perched on a knoll high above town, it's a wonderful place to stay for immersion in Berlin's past while enjoying luxurious modern amenities.

Assateague State Park on Assateague Island, just outside town, is Maryland's only oceanfront park, and it has a popular beach for surfing, sunbathing, and swimming. Wild horses roam freely on the barrier island, bordered by the Atlantic Ocean to the east and the Sinepuxent Bay to the west. It's common to see ponies feeding on marsh and dune

BERLIN MARYLAND

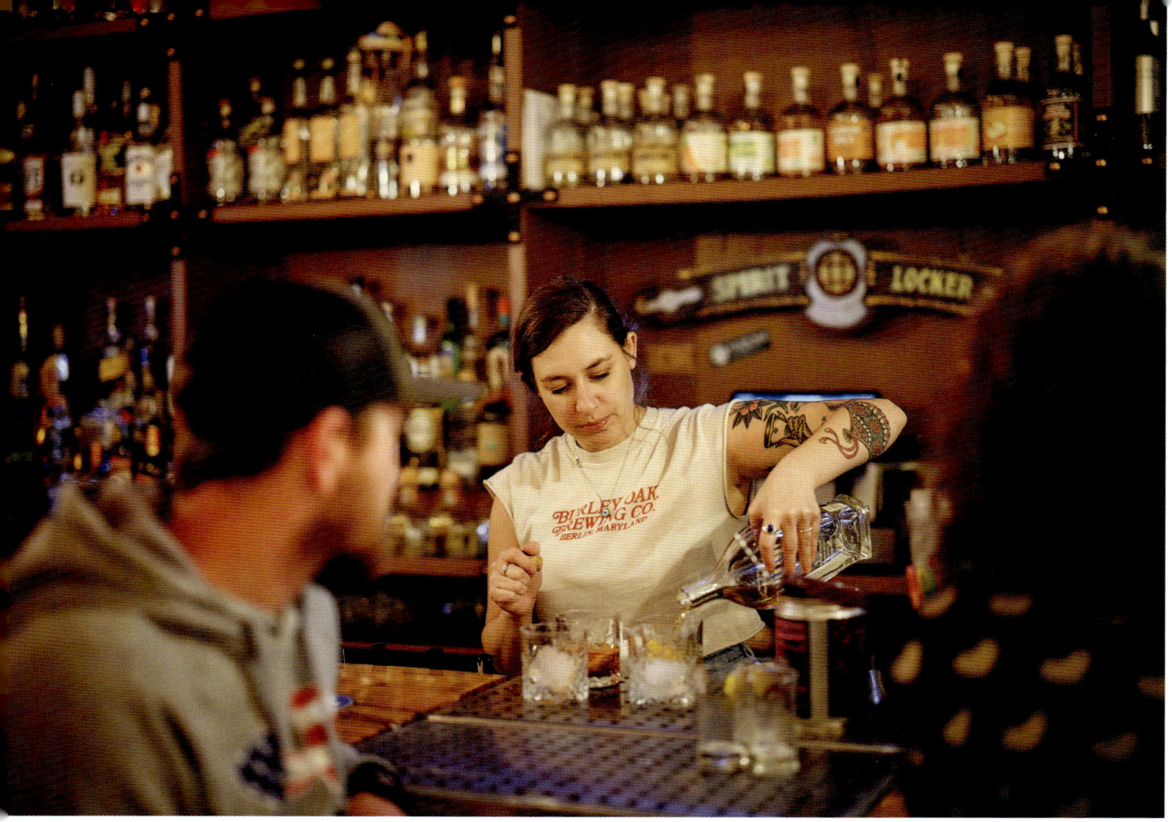
SPIRIT
LOCKER
BREWING CO.
BERLIN MARYLAND

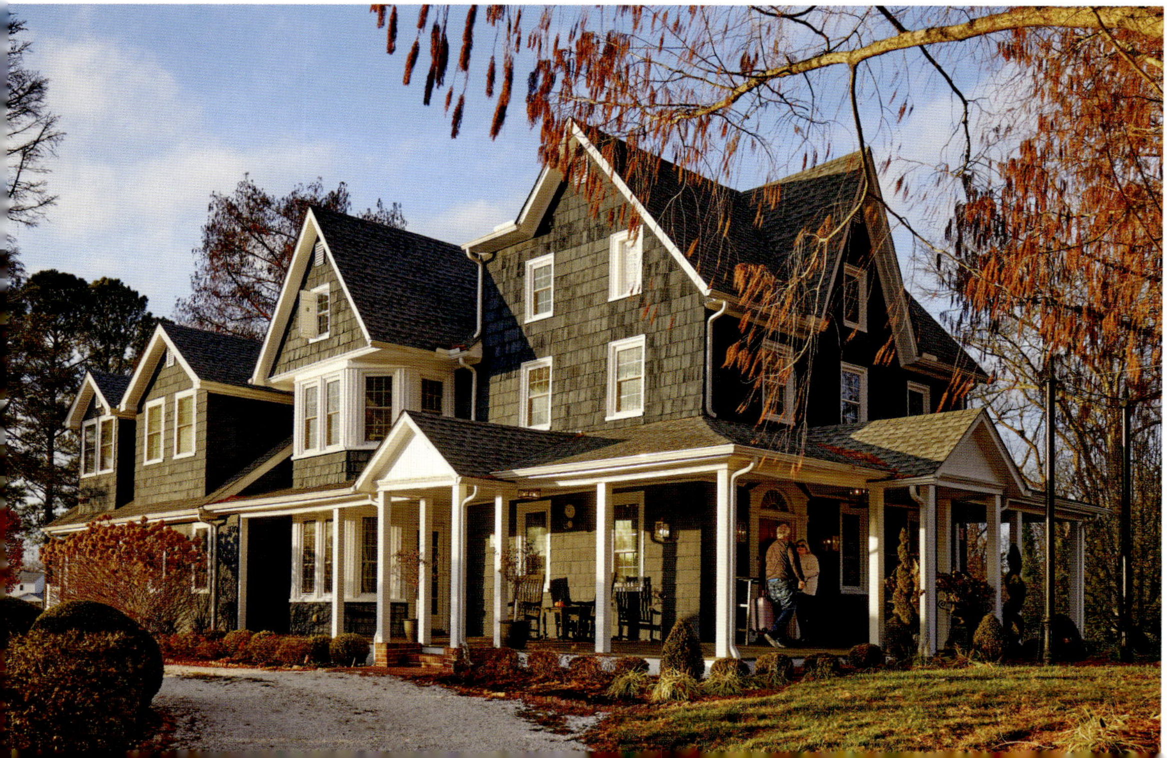

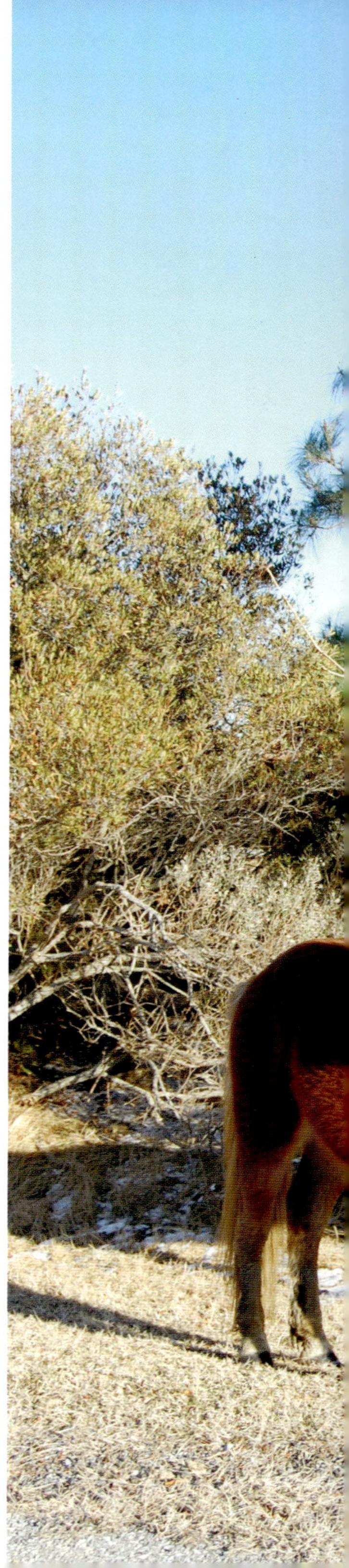

OPPOSITE TOP: Burley Oak Brewing Company offers everything from craft IPAs to canned cocktails. OPPOSITE BOTTOM: The Inn Berlin is a bed-and-breakfast with a completely gluten-free bakery. LEFT: Wild horses populate Assateague Island.

grass or frolicking in the surf; however, park rangers advise keeping a healthy distance from them. Local legend supposes that they arrived on the island from a late 18th- or early 19th-century shipwreck, or from colonial farmers looking to graze their herd tax free. Visit in July to watch the Chincoteague Pony Swim, an annual tradition where wild ponies are herded from Assateague Island on the Maryland side to Chincoteague Island on the Virginia side. The swim is put on by the Chincoteague Volunteer Fire Company, and the subsequent pony auction helps keep herd populations on the islands balanced. Any other time of year, you can kayak through the salt marshes or camp among the sandy dunes to experience the beauty of Maryland's coastline before heading back to Berlin for lunch or dinner.

TASTE OF THE REGION

SMITH ISLAND CAKE

The official dessert of Maryland is Smith Island cake, defined by its ultra-thin yellow cake stacked at least eight layers high and covered with fudge frosting. The cake dates back to the 1800s, when it was made as a symbol of community and affection, and it was often sent along with fishermen to remind them of home while on the water.

EASTON

MARYLAND

Easton, a hub of Maryland's Eastern Shore, is a foodie and art enthusiast's haven. You can build an entire trip to Easton around finding your next great meal at one of the restaurants along its historic streets. There's no shortage of places to try, from the sophisticated whiskey lounge at the Stewart to the European fine dining at Bas Rouge to the sun-filled bistro at Sunflowers and Greens. If those don't suit your mood, sample French-inspired ice cream and pies at Bonheur or gourmet artisanal fare at the wood-paneled Wardroom.

Immerse yourself in the town's history with a stay at the Tidewater Inn, which has been charming guests since 1712. The luxury bed-and-breakfast features 86 rooms as well as the Hunters' Tavern for on-site dining. Or stay at its sister property, Tidewater House, set in a circa 1874 mansion, where rooms are furnished with antique pieces in a variety of historical styles.

Downtown Easton is particularly charming in the fall, when the leaves burst with color.

Begin a day of exploring Easton's beautiful downtown at Weather Gage, a café with daily homemade pastries. From there, mosey down the brick sidewalks to Flying Cloud Booksellers, an independent bookshop with vintage posters and murals covering the walls. You'll find antique shops and galleries all along Dover Street. In fact, the Easton Arts District covers most of the historic downtown area and hosts the nationally recognized Plein Air Easton art festival each July. First Fridays bring out the art lovers in town for an extended-hours gallery walk. The Easton Farmers' Market, which claims to be the oldest continuously operating open-air farmers market in the country, sells local produce and crafts year-round.

Easton is home to the Third Meeting House, built in 1684. Despite the name, it's considered to be the oldest Quaker meeting house in the country (colonial Quakers settled throughout Maryland). For more history, bike the Easton Rail Trail to sightsee nearly the entire town on two wheels and to take in the serene, tree-filled countryside.

H.M. KRENT

ST. MICHAELS

MARYLAND

St. Michaels is known as "the town that fooled the British." Legend says that during the War of 1812, the townspeople, tipped off by the local militia, set lanterns in treetops, on ships' mastheads, and on the roofs of buildings to fool the enemy into overshooting their marks. The roof of only one home, dubbed the Cannonball House, was damaged when a cannonball crashed through and rolled down the stairs. Or so the story goes.

Set along the Chesapeake Bay on Maryland's Eastern Shore, St. Michaels wears its history on its sleeve, from the well-preserved 18th-century Victorian downtown to the crab dredgers and sailboats floating in the marina. The Chesapeake Bay Maritime Museum sits right on the waterfront. Here, you can learn about the Oyster Wars aboard an oyster-harvesting skipjack and climb to the top of the 1879 Hooper Strait Lighthouse. The Crab Claw is a favored waterfront restaurant and a local landmark housed in an old clam-and-oyster-shucking house. There's no better place to enjoy hot steamed blue crabs and a cold beer along the Miles River than its dockside patio.

You can spend most of a day here on the water, on a boat, kayak, canoe, or paddleboard. On land, there are miles of countryside to explore, like the bike routes along the Hunting Creek tributary that wind through coastal architecture and farmland. Cruise down South Talbot Street to take in lovely boutiques, quirky antique shops, ice-cream parlors, and seafood restaurants.

Boats can dock right in front of the Chesapeake Bay Maritime Museum—ideal real estate for one of the museum's many festivals throughout the year.

TASTE OF THE REGION

MARYLAND BLUE CRAB

The blue crab is Maryland's official state crustacean, famous for its blue claws, which turn a bright red-orange after cooking. Classic fare for the Chesapeake region is a bushel of Maryland blue crabs steamed to tender perfection, seasoned with a generous amount of Old Bay, and served family style with corn on the cob and melted butter on the side.

OAK BLUFFS

MASSACHUSETTS

The brilliant sunsets seen from Oak Bluffs' Ocean Park are unmatched, except perhaps by the fuchsia, turquoise, and tangerine of the famous gingerbread cottages lining the town. These 19th-century houses sprang from Methodist camp meetings—the area is still called "the Campground"—and today they're an iconic feature of Oak Bluffs. The stained-glass windows of the Campground Tabernacle, which dates to the early 1800s and is now a national historic landmark, rise above the town. For one night each August, the whole Campground, from the cottages to the tabernacle, is alight with paper lanterns during Grand Illumination Night.

Oak Bluffs sits on the northeast shore of Martha's Vineyard, on land originally inhabited by the Wampanoag people. During the late 1700s and throughout the 1800s, the area became a hub for the whaling and fishing industries. Many Black men advanced within the fishing industry, particularly with the purchase of a seaman's protection certificate, which, beginning in 1796, served as proof they were free rather than enslaved. Black whaling captains bought up many prominent plots of land in Oak Bluffs. In 1912, the Inn at Shearer Cottage opened as the first inn for Black vacationers. The inn buzzed with affluent African Americans, as well as famous writers and singers, many of whom made their way to Oak Bluffs on summer vacations from sweltering New York during the Harlem Renaissance. In recent

Each summer, Oak Bluffs residents display Chinese and Japanese lanterns outside their homes, lighting them all at once on Grand Illumination Night.

TALK LIKE A LOCAL

"THE VINEYARD"

When planning a vacation to the incomparable Martha's Vineyard, know you are going for a stay "on" the Vineyard, not "at" or "to" or "in." Get the lingo down to sound like an official islander. And remember that there are no operating vineyards on the island, which instead gets its name from Martha, the daughter of British explorer Bartholomew Gosnold, and the brambly vines that grow along the shoreline.

Every morning, members of the Inkwell Polar Bears swim group brave the freezing waters of Inkwell Beach.

years, President Barack Obama and First Lady Michelle Obama purchased a home overlooking the water, cementing the importance of this place in modern American history. You can tour the African American Heritage Trail to see notable locations throughout town.

Pedal a beach cruiser around the island to explore like a local. Or head along the many bike paths crisscrossing the landscape to East Chop Lighthouse or rural Chappaquiddick Island, called Chappy for short. The hardest decision you'll make while vacationing in Oak Bluffs is deciding which beach to visit. Inkwell Beach, located within walking distance of the ferry port, fills with sunbathers throughout the summer. The Inkwell Polar Bears, a daily swim group started in the 1940s, meet here every morning. Joseph Sylvia State Beach is another popular spot, with a gradual drop-off in the water and often gentler waves. The iconic 1975 movie *Jaws* was filmed here, and it's common to see kids and adults jumping into the ocean from what's now known as the Jaws Bridge. Rent paddleboards or kayaks to explore Sengekontacket Pond.

In the heart of Oak Bluffs is Circuit Avenue, a one-way street lined with restaurants, cafés, and shops. Mocha Mott's is a well-loved café that is packed each morning with early risers looking for a caffeine jolt and a bagel. More adventurous eaters can sample the lobster ice cream at Ben & Bill's Chocolate Emporium. Down by the pier is Nancy's Restaurant,

OPPOSITE TOP: Gingerbread cottages line the Campground. **OPPOSITE BOTTOM:** Parts of Lagoon Pond, a watershed shared by Oak Bluffs and Tisbury, Massachusetts, are open for shellfishing. **LEFT:** Oak Bluffs' Grand Illumination Night celebration includes a fireworks display.

a Martha's Vineyard institution. Its boardwalk patio is filled daily with patrons enjoying lobster rolls and Nancy's famous Dirty Banana frozen cocktail (a play on a mudslide). The Pawnee House restaurant, set in what remains of a portion of an 1872 Victorian hotel, serves modern comfort food from chicken pot pie to a falafel burger bowl. Or grab a bite from Coop de Ville, a dockside seafood shack with fried clams, lobster platters, and steamers.

The Alison Shaw Gallery, near the center of town, displays the work of the prominent photographer, known for capturing scenes of the island. For decades, Oak Bluffs has won the hearts of visitors with its coastal environment and laid-back atmosphere. Let it win over yours.

ADVENTURE ALONG THE WAY

AQUINNAH CLIFFS

The red clay Aquinnah Cliffs on the southwestern tip of Martha's Vineyard were carved by glaciers eons ago. The sacred clay that makes up the cliffs is the property of the local Wampanoag Tribe of Gay Head (Aquinnah). Pathways along Moshup Beach give visitors a chance to explore the cliffs up close, and hikes along the bluffs provide scenic vistas of Gay Head Lighthouse. Sunsets are spectacular as the colors blaze along the sandy shores.

LOBSTER
POT
PUBLIC PEDESTRIAN ACCESS
Lagosta na Panela
AIR CONDITIONED WATERFRONT DINING
WATERFRONT DINING
ATM
RAW BAR
OPEN

PROVINCETOWN

MASSACHUSETTS

History books tell the story wrong: When the pilgrims first arrived on the shores of what is now the United States in November 1620, they *first* landed in Provincetown—not Plymouth Rock. After signing the Mayflower Compact, they sailed across the bay to the more fertile environment of Plymouth. To commemorate the real landing, Provincetown's Pilgrim Monument soars 252 feet into the sky and is the tallest all-granite structure in the country—an apt homage to the town's role in U.S. history.

Known as P-town to locals, Provincetown sits at the northern tip of Cape Cod. It's a laid-back coastal community that embraces people from all walks of life. In the 1600s, it was called Helltown for its reputation as a haven for gamblers, pirates, and smugglers. But today, there's a harmonious mix between the local fishing industry and the arts. The town has fostered artists for more than 100 years and remains the oldest continuous art colony in the country. Museums, art galleries, and theaters line the streets. The bohemian culture has attracted and been nurtured by the LGBTQIA+ community, with celebratory events and festivals like Holly Folly in December and Carnival in August. P-town is known to welcome everyone.

Beloved indie shops line Commercial Street and the downtown area, like Marine Specialties, aka the "Army Navy Store," which has been a flagship of P-town for more than 50 years. Bayside restaurants are packed each evening: Try the Mews Restaurant and Cafe overlooking the harbor or the Lobster Pot by the pier. Beachy activities are a daytime staple. Race Point Beach is home to the Old Harbor Life-Saving Station Museum, while Herring Cove Beach on Cape Cod Bay offers gentler waves—a perfect spot to sun and splash.

The aptly named White Porch Inn offers a charming place to rest your head, modern amenities within steps of the beach, and a curated collection of modern art. Enjoy coffee or wine on its iconic front porch while watching the action pass by on Johnson Street.

The Lobster Pot, family-owned since 1979, offers Cape Cod seafood staples. Can't make the trip? They ship their chowder nationwide.

STOCKBRIDGE

MASSACHUSETTS

Winding roads lined with dense forests and rolling hills lead the way into Stockbridge, a quintessential New England town of about 2,000 permanent residents. A gateway to the Berkshires, Stockbridge is filled with charm and history. Notably, the Red Lion Inn on Main Street dates back to 1773 and is one of the few American inns that has operated continuously since before the Revolutionary War. Its interiors are adorned with famous colonial antiques, and the large front porch is filled with rocking chairs and wicker love seats, beckoning guests to stay awhile—perhaps with a glass of wine. Choose a room in the main inn or stay in one of the guest cottages as a base camp for exploring the many shops and restaurants within walking distance. Through the years, patrons of the Red Lion Inn have included presidents, famous musicians and actors, and acclaimed novelists. Don't forget to grab a lunch or dinner of hearty sandwiches and soups at Widow Bingham's Tavern, named after one of the inn's original owners.

Other significant historical sites include the Norman Rockwell Museum and Naumkeag, a public garden and museum that was a summer home for noted New York City attorney and U.S. ambassador Joseph Hodges Choate and his family during the Gilded Age. Explore the town's nooks and crannies to discover places like Lost Lamb, a "French-Berkshire fusion patisserie," and the Mews, an alleyway filled with restaurants and shops. For an outdoorsy day, go hiking in the Berkshires or kayaking on Stockbridge Bowl (Lake Mahkeenac).

The best time to visit Stockbridge is on the weekend or during a festival, when local pride is most prominent. Time your visit to the Harvest Fest at the Berkshire Botanical Gardens in fall, the springtime Daffodil and Tulip Festival, or the wintertime Winterlights at Naumkeag. For theater and performing arts entertainment, the Berkshire Theatre Group packs local stages such as the Colonial Theatre, the Unicorn Theatre, and the Fitzpatrick Main Stage most weekends.

The Blue Steps rank among the most-photographed sites at Naumkeag, a historic 19th-century estate in Stockbridge.

LITTLETON

NEW HAMPSHIRE

"Be glad" is tossed around like a greeting or farewell in Littleton. It harks back to resident Eleanor H. Porter's 1913 literary classic *Pollyanna*. Porter's cheerful protagonist is immortalized in a bronze statue in front of the Littleton Library on Main Street, with arms flung wide to welcome all who pass by. You can't help feeling optimistic yourself while visiting this small New Hampshire town. There's a sense of community and pride among residents and local business owners. The town is extremely walkable, with unique art galleries, craft breweries, and inviting cafés lining Main and Mill Streets in the River District. The winding gravel Riverwalk crosses a 230-foot-long covered bridge and the Ammonoosuc River and provides an excellent walking route for a tour of town and the beautiful surrounding landscape.

Schilling Beer Company serves small-batch European-inspired beer in a renovated three-story 1797 gristmill. Its cheery patio overlooking the river is the place to be on a weekend afternoon or evening. Chutters holds the title of the world's longest candy counter and offers a slew of nostalgic sweet treats. Chang Thai Cafe, an award-winning restaurant in the heart of town, strives to represent the virtues of its namesake—*chang* means "elephant" in Thai—with good fortune and friendliness behind every dish. The historic downtown Thayers Inn originally opened in 1850 as the Thayer's White

Franconia Notch State Park has numerous camping sites from which you can embark on a hike through the fall foliage.

ADVENTURE ALONG THE WAY

KANCAMAGUS SCENIC BYWAY

Visitors flock to the Kancamagus Scenic Byway—or as those in the know call it, the Kanc—for some of the best leaf-peeping in the country. Designated a national scenic byway, the Kanc stretches 34.5 miles through White Mountain National Forest in northern New Hampshire. The byway route takes drivers past Sabbaday Falls, Rocky Gorge, and the Swift River, a true buffet of incredible New England landscapes. Campsites dot the wilderness, and red spruce, beech, and hemlock trees create a lush forest ready for exploration.

Chutters candy store on Main Street boasts a 112-foot candy counter—the world's longest—lined with glass jars containing more than 700 different kinds of sweets.

Mountain Hotel. Today, it's a cozy stay that puts you in the center of the action.

Littleton often serves as a base camp for those looking to explore the White Mountains, which sit to the west of town. Franconia Notch State Park, located in White Mountains National Forest, is just a short drive south. The park's popular Artists Bluff Trail, a 1.4-mile loop around Echo Lake (a wonderful spot for swimming, fishing, or kayaking), provides fantastic mountain views. For those wanting a more relaxed way to take in the spectacular scenery, especially during the fall foliage season, climb aboard the park's aerial tram at Cannon Mountain, which is typically open between May and October. The scenic boardwalk along Flume Gorge is another great option for views. Rushing waterfalls, covered bridges, 70-foot granite walls, and views of Mount Liberty nearly steal the show from the impressive moss-covered Conway rock face.

TALK LIKE A LOCAL

"FRAPPE"

When most of us order a frappe, we're expecting an icy coffee or espresso drink. Not so in New Hampshire, or most of New England, for that matter. New Englanders use "frappe" as a term for a milkshake—the creamy kind made with ice cream.

ROCK YOU
YOUR LOVE
HIGHER
THAN I'VE EVER BEEN LIFTED BEFORE
SWEET & SILKY CANDY CHEWS
HAPPY
Jelly Belly

PORTSMOUTH

NEW HAMPSHIRE

An hour north of Boston, the charming littoral settlement of Portsmouth is one of the earliest seaports in North America and the oldest city in New Hampshire. Portsmouth blends history with cultural vibrancy in a way that makes visitors want to return again and again.

Brick and slate buildings from the 18th and 19th centuries line the town's seaport. A salty breeze comes off the Piscataqua River, water laps at the wooden piers and rocky seawalls, and the ocean is your backdrop for boutique shopping on the cobblestone streets off Market Square (no sales tax in the state doesn't hurt, either). Portsmouth's award-winning restaurants are so numerous that the town boasts having more seats to dine in than residents to occupy them. There's lobster, maritime history, nationally recognized breweries, and a vibrant performing arts scene—the makings of a perfect New Hampshire getaway.

Portsmouth calls back to the days of coastal colonial living, from its tall clock towers to brightly painted homes and hulls.

History buffs should begin at the Strawbery Banke Museum, where artifacts such as pottery, stone tools, and traditionally built wigwam frames share the story of the Abenaki people who visited the seacoast seasonally for more than 12,000 years. Today, this living museum spans 10 acres and includes historical gardens and 32 standing properties that showcase life through the ages in a Portsmouth neighborhood, blending the precolonial times of the Abenaki, the colonial era, and the 1950s. Living historians role-play in costume around

TASTE OF THE REGION

POPOVER

Sharing many similarities with Great Britain's Yorkshire pudding, the light, eggy popover gets its name from how it nearly pops out of the dish during the baking process. It is crispy on the outside and melt-in-your-mouth flaky on the inside. Portsmouth's Popovers on the Square serves the classic New England pastry with a house-made maple butter, but it's just as delicious plain.

The Portsmouth African Burying Ground Memorial Park marks the 18th-century gravesite of nearly 200 freed and enslaved Africans.

the museum, giving demonstrations on cooking by hearth, barrelmaking, and weaving. The name of the museum is history in its own right: Portsmouth was originally called Strawbery Banke for the abundant wild strawberries that grew along the Piscataqua River. Keep an eye out for them while exploring the area today.

The Portsmouth Harbour Trail continues the history lesson as it winds past dozens of landmarks. The town's location on the river made it a prime fishing and shipbuilding center after colonial settlers arrived in 1623. In the 20th century, the local industry shifted toward building and repairing submarines, a trade you can learn more about at Albacore Park, home of the U.S.S. *Albacore*, a decommissioned submarine that now serves as a museum. Today, fishing remains an integral part of life. At Geno's, a dockside institution, patrons have a front-row seat as the catch of the day is loaded directly from the lobster boats to the restaurant's back deck.

Walking Portsmouth's Black Heritage Trail offers a different perspective on the town's early days. New Hampshire was one of the few American colonies that did not impose tariffs on enslaved people, so thousands of enslaved Africans passed through the port in the late 17th and early 18th centuries. Today, Chestnut Street is the site of the African Burying Ground Memorial Park, built on the site of a once forgotten cemetery for enslaved

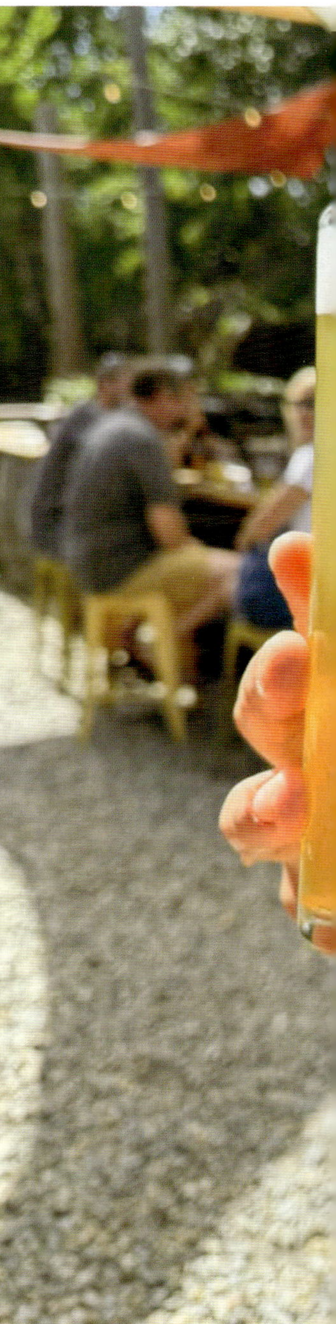

OPPOSITE TOP: Peek below the docks on Peirce Island to spot sea stars. OPPOSITE BOTTOM: Play old-timey games at the Strawbery Banke Museum. LEFT: Loaded Question Brewing on Islington Street offers craft beer as well as local hard ciders and seltzers.

people, a poignant reminder of the hands that built the city and the suffering wrought by the slave trade.

History and preservation mark one side of Portsmouth's passion. The other is excellent craft beer. New Hampshire regularly ranks first among states in beer consumption per capita, so it's no surprise that a handful of award-winning breweries can be found in Portsmouth. In February, you can try a bevy of local brews during Seacoast Beer Week, a celebration of beloved breweries from New Hampshire and Maine with events throughout town. Other times of the year you can stop in to sample what's on tap at local favorites like Loaded Question Brewing and Liars Bench Beer Company.

ADVENTURE ALONG THE WAY

ISLES OF SHOALS

Sail six miles out of Portsmouth Harbor to reach the Isles of Shoals, a group of nine rocky islands that were occupied by fishing communities in the 1600s and 1700s. The private moorings of Gosport Harbor are sheltered by four of the islands—Cedar, Smuttynose, Star, and Malaga—but all nine islands are worth exploring from the bow of a boat. Terns fly overhead near Seavey Island, White Island's lighthouse rises tall, and sunbathing seals fill the ledges at Duck Island.

931
Beach
GUEST HOUSE
(609) 884-0275

CAPE MAY

NEW JERSEY

From outdoor offerings to historic landmarks, Cape May, at the southernmost point in New Jersey, lives up to its reputation as America's original seaside resort town. (It's been a popular beach retreat since the 1700s.) The vibrant Victorian homes that line Beach Avenue are the coastal town's trademark. The beachfront homes were rebuilt after a fire devastated 30 blocks of town in 1878. Restoration efforts by preservationists in the late 20th century helped revive the town's historic architecture and earned Cape May a designation as a national historic landmark. Today, it has the second highest concentration of Victorian homes in the country, after San Francisco.

One stop worth making is the Emlen Physick Estate, a house museum demonstrating Victorian Stick-style architecture and family life in 1879. Also worthwhile is the Harriet Tubman Museum, in the historic Howell House, which pays tribute to the abolitionist activist who lived in Cape May in the early 1850s. The museum also honors the town's role in the Underground Railroad. Take a trolley tour through the historic district or past the seaside mansions for a ride that brings the town's heritage to life.

Other Victorians have been converted into charming bed-and-breakfasts and boutique hotels. For instance, the Mooring, one block from the beach, has been welcoming guests since 1882. The renovated Mason Cottage Bed and Breakfast, a

Cape May's Victorian architecture is a signature of the resort town.

TASTE OF THE REGION

PORK ROLL SANDWICH

The official sandwich of New Jersey is the pork roll (aka Taylor ham) sandwich, most often enjoyed as a breakfast item. Pork roll is similar to bologna or Spam—a cured, smoked, precooked pork product. Crispy layers of pork roll are mixed with egg and cheese and served on a hard roll (or, if you prefer, a bagel). Originating in the city of Trenton, two hours north of Cape May, it's gone statewide. There is even a pork roll festival to celebrate the Garden State's favorite meat.

The Lobster House, overlooking Cape May Harbor, offers lobsters as meaty as three pounds, steamed or broiled. (You can ask your server if larger sizes are available.)

Victorian home built in 1871, sits in the downtown historic district.

Iconic red-and-white lifeguard towers dot the sandy beaches that run parallel to town. The Cove, at the end of the promenade, is one of the most popular spots for swimming in the surf, building sandcastles, and basking in the sun. In Cape May Point State Park, you can climb the 199 steps of the original cast-iron spiral staircase to the top of Cape May Lighthouse, opened in 1859, for panoramic views of Delaware Bay and the Atlantic Ocean.

Come fall, thousands of songbirds make a brief migratory flight up the Delaware Bayshore Byway. Make your way to Higbee Beach just before the sun crests over the horizon to witness what the New Jersey Audubon Society calls "morning flight," as thousands of feathered creatures take to the sky. The Cape May Bird Observatory coordinates some of the best migration-watching in the world. The peninsula serves as an ideal natural funnel for the flight patterns of hundreds of thousands of seabirds.

Head to the harbor to grab a cocktail at the lounge on the Schooner *American*—an authentic Grand Banks sailing vessel moored dockside—and fresh seafood at the Lobster House. Inland, a tree-lined gravel road transports visitors to the magical acreage of Beach Plum Farm. Fluffy, candy-colored hydrangeas line the gardens surrounding the rustic

SPRING
FISH & SUPPLY COMPANY
Wholesale Fish and Scallop Dealers
EST 1922

OPPOSITE TOP: Sanderlings swoop over Cape May during the spring migration. **OPPOSITE BOTTOM:** Cyclists enjoy the promenade at Cove Beach. **LEFT:** Shop for farm-to-table goods or dine among the gardens of Beach Plum Farm.

yet elegant Amish barn that serves as a daily market for farm-fresh foods and curated goods, as well as a restaurant called Farm Kitchen. Tickets for its year-round farm-to-table dinner series sell out quickly. Plan ahead to book a seat at the Summer Harvest, set under café lights and green umbrellas and surrounded by lavender and honeysuckle fields, or at a Holiday Dinner, set in the cedar-garland-strewn hoop house, complete with a candlelight garden stroll. A visit to the working farm celebrates the agricultural heritage of New Jersey and offers a different perspective from the town's bustling beaches. The harvests yielded at Beach Plum Farm provide produce and meats to many local Cape May restaurants. For a truly immersive experience, stay at one of the six historic cottages and barns on the property.

TASTE OF THE REGION

WATER ICE

A summertime visit to the Jersey shore isn't complete without a water ice to cool off following an afternoon at the beach. Sometimes called Italian ice, it is somewhere between a slushie and a snow cone and is flavored with fruity, tangy flavors like lemon, cherry, watermelon, or mango. This frozen treat originated in Italy and was brought to the States by immigrants in the early 1920s.

LAMBERTVILLE

NEW JERSEY

The Garden State moniker rings true as you traverse the pastoral countryside of southwestern Hunterdon County. Rolling hills abound, and verdant white oak, river birch, and shagbark hickory trees line the Delaware River. A stately iron bridge crosses the water, connecting Lambertville to New Hope, Pennsylvania. On the Lambertville side, you'll find renowned antique shops and tons of character.

The Antiques Capital of New Jersey, Lambertville appeals to serious collectors and casual browsers alike. The four-story Antiques Center at the People's Store on North Union Street houses more than 50 dealers, and the Golden Nugget Antique Flea Market is a 50-year Lambertville institution with open-air tables. Both are a must-visit while in town. Stroll down Bridge Street for more shopping, and for a refreshment stop at Boat House, a nautical carriage house bar with beer steins hanging from the rafters, or Savour, a cheese shop with gourmet provisions.

Numerous antique dealers call Lambertville home. Look for their shops on Union Street.

Lambertville was once an industrial center with factories that churned out patented "Snag-proof" rubber boots, porcelain toilets, wagon wheels, and 15 tons of hairpins per week. The Delaware and Raritan Canal was constructed to transport the goods, but it was abandoned by the Pennsylvania Railroad Company in 1937. Today, the canal is D&R Canal State Park, with a tree-lined walking and biking path along the river. For panoramic views of the area, hike up the winding forested trail to Goat Hill Overlook.

ADVENTURE ALONG THE WAY

WASHINGTON CROSSING STATE PARK

Downriver from Lambertville is the site of the famous 1776 George Washington Christmas Day Delaware River crossing that turned the tide of the Revolutionary War and reignited the cause of freedom. Washington Crossing State Park is set on 500 beautiful acres and features reenactments of the famed crossing, a historic village with preserved buildings from the late 1700s and early 1800s, and Bowman's Hill Tower, a stone lookout that rises above the tree line and provides sweeping views of the countryside and the river.

BEACON

NEW YORK

The roar of Fishkill Falls is a constant background sound for visitors exploring downtown Beacon. Along Main Street's mile of ancient brick buildings are several former hat factories that gave it renown as the hatmaking capital of the United States. Today, the buildings have been repurposed into boutiques, cafés, and restaurants. One of the most compelling is the Roundhouse. Formerly part of the Matteawan Manufacturing Company, a top hat-textile manufacturer, it is now a stunning complex consisting of a hotel, a restaurant, and an event center. Dine on a deck overlooking Fishkill Falls or, during colder months, inside an industrial turret with floor-to-ceiling windows.

Begin your morning with fresh bagels and muffins served outside your door at the hotel portion of the Roundhouse. Then set off on a walk along Scenic Hudson's Long Dock Park, a riverfront trail with offshoot paths, a kayak launchpad, and benches and picnic tables. Fishermen dot the boardwalk, and it's a peaceful place to watch the sunrise on the river. Take a five-minute drive down the road to Dia Beacon. This world-renowned modern art museum, opened in 2003 inside the old National Biscuit Carton Making and Printing Plant (better known as Nabisco) on the banks of the Hudson River, was a pioneer in preserving and converting industrial buildings for contemporary use. Finish your day by going to a come-and-go bonfire along the riverfront, a popular activity for locals.

Other historic sites worth visiting include the Madam Brett Homestead, the oldest standing

The Dia Beacon museum showcases works from sculptor Richard Serra's "Torqued Ellipses" series.

ADVENTURE ALONG THE WAY

ANGRY ORCHARD CIDER HOUSE

The Angry Orchard Cider House, in Walden, New York (30 minutes west of Beacon), is a must-visit for cider fans. Its sprawling property has firepits and games, and café lights strung around the apple orchards as a warm welcome to the Hudson Valley. Set up a private tasting in a tree house to sample a selection of refreshing hard ciders.

Visitors to Bannerman Castle can tour the grounds via a boat ride and walking tour.

building in Dutchess County. Catheryna Rombout Brett has been called America's first female real estate tycoon and is credited with developing the entire area by selling off parcels of her nearly 30,000-acre estate (rather than renting, which was much more common at the time) after being widowed at the age of 31. Her 1709 home is maintained by the Daughters of the American Revolution and features original scallop shingles, a Dutch door, and sloping dormers. Also worthwhile is Bannerman Castle, on Pollepel Island in the middle of the Hudson River. You can rent a canoe or kayak to reach the island or take a cruise with a guided walking tour; either way offers insight and views of the 1917 Scottish-inspired castle ruins.

Modern delights abound in Beacon, too, particularly when it comes to food. Stroll through the Hudson Valley Food Hall, an international dining venue with stalls offering everything from barbecue to Middle Eastern cuisine. For breakfast, head to Beacon Bread Company, a cozy spot where strawberry cannoli griddles (pancakes stuffed with strawberries and sweet whipped ricotta) share the menu with chicken and waffles. Later, sip your way into the evening at Denning's Point Distillery, housed downtown in a 19th-century building. Or end the night with something sweet at Five Pennies Creamery, where you can choose from more than 100 flavors of ice cream made on-site (don't forget to order yours in a homemade waffle cone).

SAFE AT HOME
BALLPARK
COLLECTIBLES
"A life is not important
in the impact it has on o
-Jackie Robinson
Silver
GIFT
SHOP
Fox
WHERE IT ALL BEG
BAT CO.
BAT CO.
Choose Your Favorite
Wood Bat
FIELDS
NEW ERA

COOPERSTOWN

NEW YORK

Clear blue Otsego Lake is the visual centerpiece of Cooperstown, in the Catskills region of New York. Cooperstown became a popular summer retreat in the 1800s for those looking to escape the heat of New York City. The town's charm-infused fame came thanks to its pastoral beauty, which drew the attention of writers of the era, as well as publisher Elihu Phinney, who set up a printing press right in town, supplying locals with newspapers and almanacs.

Today, Cooperstown is perhaps most famously known as the home of the National Baseball Hall of Fame and Museum, located on Main Street. Abner Doubleday, the purported inventor of baseball, reportedly hosted the first ever baseball game on a lot on Elihu Phinney's property (now the location of Doubleday Field) in 1839. While that claim has since been debunked, Cooperstown's legendary role in the world of baseball endures. It's worth visiting both the museum and the field to learn about the impact America's national pastime has had in shaping the nation and to see memorabilia from the sport's most legendary games and figures.

Walk Cooperstown's Main Street to visit numerous galleries and boutiques, as well as the Baseball Hall of Fame.

To explore the rest of town, hop on the Trolley System, with its five old-fashioned trolleys that zip you between an eclectic mix of shops and restaurants. The Smithy, built in 1786, is the oldest building in town and now home to a gallery and clay studio. Tin Bin Alley is filled with nostalgic candy and store-made fudge. Complete the Cooperstown Beverage Trail by visiting its eight craft-beverage establishments, including local favorites Brewery Ommegang and Fly Creek Cider Mill and Orchard. The Otesaga Resort Hotel, built in 1909, is

TALK LIKE A LOCAL

"GOING TO CAMP"

For the rest of the country, going to camp means spending a youthful summer at outdoor wilderness camps. For some New Yorkers, it means traveling to a family's upstate lake house or summer rental to escape the brutal heat and humidity pervasive in the city.

Take in Lake Otsego at Lakefront Park, a few minutes' walk from downtown.

an iconic representation of Cooperstown's history. Recently fully restored, the resort is a member of the Historic Hotels of America program and on the National Register of Historic Places. Its refined elegance and gracious hospitality make it as much of a draw today as it was when it first opened. The grand federal-style brick building sits near the water, with a patio overlooking Otsego Lake and the bucolic countryside. Its Leatherstocking Golf Course, one of the best courses on the East Coast, lures golfers with its challenging track and scenery along the lake.

Author James Fenimore Cooper, the son of town founder William Cooper, is best known for his 1826 novel *The Last of the Mohicans*. But it was his *Leatherstocking Tales* series—which features stories based in and around Cooperstown—that gave Otsego Lake the nickname Glimmerglass. The Glimmerglass Festival, a summerlong celebration of the arts, hosts operas and musicals in a lakeside venue. Glimmerglass State Park, just north of town, overlooks Otsego Lake and offers picturesque hiking and biking trails including worthwhile Beaver Pond and Sleeping Lion. Council Rock Park has an incredible view of the lake and commemorates the people of the Haudenosaunee Confederacy, who lived on this land for millennia, with a historical marker at the entrance to the park.

HUDSON

NEW YORK

Walk down Warren Street in the heart of Hudson for a selection of award-winning restaurants to try, boutiques to shop, and galleries to gawk in. This small town, about an hour and a half north of New York City, has been dubbed the "Brooklyn of the Hudson Valley" because so many former city dwellers have flocked to this cultural, artisanal, and artistic enclave along the Hudson River. The dining scene holds its own against the Big Apple's, with innovative concepts like Feast & Floret, which serves seasonal Italian fare among make-your-own flower bouquets, and Le Perche Bakery & Bar, a French eatery housed in a 19th-century town house.

A favorite spot downtown is the Antique Warehouse, a mecca of antique shops and stalls with a brewery next door. Historic buildings throughout Hudson have been repurposed for modern use, like the Maker, an 1800s-era carriage house turned cocktail lounge. Inside, it feels as though you've been transported back in time, with craft beverages, leather-clad walls, and velvet wingback chairs. The Wick, a boutique hotel tucked inside a reimagined candle factory, strikes a graceful balance between heritage and contemporary style. Also in town is the FASNY (Firefighters Association of the State of New York) Museum of Firefighting, a fantastic interactive museum that pays homage to first responders throughout the United States.

For a step off the beaten path, drive 10 minutes from downtown to visit Olana State Historic Site, the beautiful home and grounds of famous landscape artist Frederic Church, a pioneer of the mid-19th-century Hudson River school. This art movement showcased the natural world before photography or leisure travel became popular. It's worthwhile to book the two-hour Olana grounds and home walking tour to learn more about the impact that Church had on the art world and to take in the views of the Hudson River Valley. If the art so inspires you, hike one of the trails across the water for a more intimate nature experience in the Catskills.

Olana State Historic Site, with its iconic 19th-century villa, is a 10-minute drive from downtown Hudson.

SARANAC LAKE

NEW YORK

The Adirondack region in upstate New York is well known for its vast smattering of lakes and ponds inside the circular chain of the eponymous mountains. Saranac Lake, a casual and high-style small town in the area, represents the past and present offerings of summer recreation.

Outdoor recreation and the charm of the postcard-perfect town draw crowds each year, particularly in the summer. The brick-paved Riverwalk, a one-mile round-trip along the Saranac River, is the best way to take in the historic downtown with coffee or pastry in hand. Or you can paddleboard, kayak, or fish on the river itself. For more high-flying adventure, scale the treetops along the bridges and tree houses on the Wild Walk at the Wild Center just outside town.

For a dose of history, visit the Saranac Laboratory Museum to see the region's original 19th-century health center—then known as the Trudeau Sanatorium. Dr. Edward Livingston Trudeau came to the Adirondacks in the 1870s to recover from tuberculosis, and after his astonishing improvement, he established the health resort and research center to combat the disease. Over time, cure cottages and bustling hotels dotted Saranac Lake, making it a fashionable destination for both leisure and health care.

Around town, you'll see sturdy Adirondack chairs—invented by designer Thomas Lee while visiting the region in 1903—on most decks and patios. Enjoy a day on Lake Flower, a meal at Campfire Adirondack Grill, and a visit to the music shop Ampersound before watching the sun set behind the lush hilltops and clear lake waters.

Book a stay at the Branch Farm Bed and Breakfast, which overlooks Lake Flower. The cozy inn is within walking distance of the Village of Saranac Lake—or guests can opt to paddle into town via Branch Farm's rental kayaks. Visit in the fall to see spectacular foliage from your bedroom windows or in the winter to take advantage of the cross-country skiing and snowshoe trails outside your door.

For respite from popular Middle Saranac Lake, visit relatively quiet Weller Pond to the north.

SARATOGA SPRINGS

NEW YORK

"Health, History, and Horses" is an apt slogan for the offerings of opulent Saratoga Springs. The first two aspects are a nod to the area's naturally carbonated mineral springs, the only ones of their kind east of the Rocky Mountains. These springs formed during the Paleozoic era and were used by the Mohawk people long before the arrival of European settlers. Then, in the 1800s, Saratoga Springs became the top vacation destination for health-conscious vacationers, who followed the prescription of drinking two cups of mineral water per day. Once the water was downed, guests were free to spend the rest of their days gambling, horse racing, and engaging in general debauchery and frivolity.

Health standards are a bit different today, but you can still participate in the town's historic traditions with a soak in the original cast-iron bathtubs at Roosevelt Baths and Spa, established in 1935 by President Franklin D. Roosevelt. An hour in the salty mineral-bath treatment is said to be therapeutic for pain relief, skin conditions, and circulation, among other benefits. Saratoga Spa State Park is a wonderful place to spend the rest of the day, with bike rentals available to explore the park and trails to visit all the natural mineral springs, such as Polaris and Karista. You can taste the spring water, but expect a salty and sulfuric sip.

Horse racing began in Saratoga Springs in 1863, when former boxing champion John Morrissey

Saratoga Race Course hosts horse races throughout the summer. Clubhouse seats offer clear views of the finish line (for a premium).

ADVENTURE ALONG THE WAY

NEW YORK STATE MILITARY MUSEUM AND VETERANS RESEARCH CENTER

Housing more than 25,000 artifacts from the Revolutionary War to today, the newly renovated New York State Military Museum and Veterans Research Center is housed in a former 1889 redbrick armory. It is a fascinating stop while visiting Saratoga Springs, with the largest collection of state battle flags in the country and exhibits containing nearly 2,500 oral histories of New York veterans.

At the racecourse, listen for the hand-rung bell that sounds 17 minutes before each post. The track still won't use the audio system for this announcement.

organized the area's first Thoroughbred meet. The sport became a permanent fixture shortly thereafter when Saratoga Race Course was built—it's the oldest continuously operating racetrack in the country and attracts visitors from July to September. Races are typically held five days a week through the summer, with Mondays and Tuesdays being the off days. You can enjoy breakfast on the Clubhouse Porch on summer race days and watch the horses train. In late August, the track hosts the annual Travers Stakes race, nicknamed the "Midsummer Derby," the oldest major Thoroughbred race in America.

Visit the National Museum of Racing and Hall of Fame across the street from the racetrack or stroll down Broadway back in town and pop into the boutiques that line the street. The jockey statues in front of most storefronts keep the spirit of racing alive and signify the immense pride Saratoga Springs has for its history.

At the end of Broadway sits Congress Park, filled with walking paths, ponds, and shady trees. In the center of the park is Canfield Casino, one of the most recognizable landmarks in the area. In the 1900s, horse races ended around 2:00 p.m. to accommodate the typical 2:30 p.m. dinnertime. This left an entire evening free for patrons with money to spend. John Morrissey opened what was then known as the Saratoga Club House in 1870, where each table boasted a $200 buy-in (nearly $5,000

FARMING
TOMATOES
4.00 bx
BLUEBERRIES
$5.00 pint
SPECIAL
2/9.—
SPECIAL
3/$13.80
FARM FRESH

OPPOSITE TOP: Saratoga Springs' outdoor farmers market operates on Wednesdays and Saturdays from May to October. **OPPOSITE BOTTOM:** Visit the National Museum of Racing and Hall of Fame on Union Avenue. **LEFT:** The area's famed mineral waters emerge from a fountain in Congress Park.

today)—to say nothing of the high-stakes poker room located on the second floor. Morrissey opened his club with three ironclad rules: No ladies allowed, cash only, and no locals. And he would anonymously donate money to local charities and churches to keep Canfield in the town's good graces. Today, the casino operates as an event venue and is also home to the Saratoga Springs History Museum. It's said to be haunted, and its numerous paranormal sightings made it a featured location on the television show *Ghosthunters*.

If you aren't up for gambling or ghost-hunting, step outside the casino into Congress Park to enjoy the beauty of Saratoga. The park also has a historic wooden carousel, built in 1910, that attracts young families all summer long.

TASTE OF THE REGION

HALF-MOON COOKIES

The beloved half-moon cookie—in which chocolate and vanilla fondant frosting meet in the middle of a drop cake-style treat—was made famous in the early 20th century at Hemstrought's Bakery in Utica, New York, about two hours west of Saratoga Springs. The classic black-and-white treat is a quintessential New York dessert.

READING BLUE MOUNTAIN AND NORTHERN
2013

JIM THORPE

PENNSYLVANIA

Jim Thorpe, a gateway to Pennsylvania's Pocono Mountains, was originally called Mauch Chunk, an Indigenous Lenape name meaning "bear place." In 1953, the town became the final resting place and commemoration site for one of the greatest athletes of the 20th century. To win the bid for that honor, all it had to do was change its name. The rub? Jim Thorpe, the first Native American to win an Olympic gold medal for the United States, had never set foot there.

The town of Jim Thorpe has boomed since the change. Today, it is home to beautiful historic sites and outstanding outdoor recreation. The steep, rocky outcroppings of Lehigh Gorge State Park were formed by the Lehigh River and railroad construction during the industrial revolution. Along the park's Delaware and Lehigh Trail, you'll see historic railroads, mining ruins, and pristine natural surroundings. Visit the 50-foot-tall Buttermilk Falls, or hop aboard the Lehigh Gorge Scenic Railway, which runs vintage coaches from 1917 along the ravine.

Along Broadway sits Millionaires' Row, a group of mansions built in the mid-1800s, when the railroad boom and coal-mining industries brought an influx of wealth to the area. The mansions have been converted to house inns, restaurants, and eclectic shops. The Inn at Jim Thorpe is especially beautiful, and the Harry Packer Mansion is now a charming bed-and-breakfast. Marion Hose Bar, in a restored firehouse, is a perfect spot to try a local beer.

Bike the Delaware and Lehigh Trail along the Lehigh Gorge Scenic Railway.

ADVENTURE ALONG THE WAY

BULLS HEAD PUBLIC HOUSE

Voted one of the best beer bars in the United States, Bulls Head Public House lies in the heart of small-town Lititz, two hours south of Jim Thorpe. Chandeliers hang over wood-paneled rooms, creating an atmosphere that feels both cozy and historic, like a traditional British pub. The bottle menu offers various styles and vintages from all over the world in a temperature-controlled cellar, and Cicerone-certified bartenders pour fresh pints on draft.

NARRAGANSETT

RHODE ISLAND

Narragansett gets its name from the Narragansett people who lived in the area for centuries before the arrival of European settlers. Situated on the Atlantic coast about 20 minutes from Newport, the town has a more laid-back, surfer-town vibe than its opulent neighbor. Narragansett is filled with weather-worn shingled homes evocative of a quintessential East Coast beach town. Rent beach cruisers to explore the shore path and the beautiful neighborhoods along the water. The Towers, the town's most notable architectural landmark and all that's left of the once glamorous Narragansett Pier Casino, will keep you oriented. It hosts free and ticketed live events throughout the year.

A short drive from the water is Matunuck Oyster Bar. Named one of the top 10 oyster bars in the world by *USA Today,* Matunuck sources from its own oyster farm and is a pioneer in sustainably farming the mollusks. The restaurant suffered a disastrous fire in 2025, but it is rebuilding. In the meantime, Matunuck offers seasonal outdoor dining beneath a tent. It's a truly special experience to eat here, enjoying freshly shucked oysters and martinis while overlooking the water.

The best time to visit Narragansett is during the summer season, typically the beginning of May through the end of September, when seasonal businesses are open and the town is most active. Make sure to end your day on an Adirondack chair overlooking the water. You'll likely to be treated to views of an unmatched summer sunset.

The 19th-century Towers, on Ocean Road, is a landmark of the town.

TASTE OF THE REGION

CLAM STUFFIE

Quahogs, a highly nutritious hard clam, are plucked straight from the waters of Rhode Island and used in many local seafood recipes. The Rhode Island stuffie is a mix of chopped quahog and sometimes sausage, spices, and breading, baked in the shell and served with a squeeze of lemon. You can find stuffies at most seafood shacks around the state, as well as on some fine-dining menus.

STOWE

VERMONT

In the shadows of Mount Mansfield, the highest peak in Vermont, is the quaint town of Stowe. While it's a place that wows in all four seasons, the snowy winter months are particularly splendid. Stowe Mountain Resort is a premier East Coast ski destination with plenty of bluebird days and challenging slopes. The ski resort is split between two peaks—Mount Mansfield and Spruce Peak—with 116 ski runs between them, 12 chairlifts, and a gondola connecting the two mountains. Start the morning on fresh legs on the Mount Mansfield side at the infamous Front Four, a collection of runs developed in the 1930s when alpine skiing first came to the mountain. These double black diamonds are not for the faint of heart; however, you'll find plenty of accessible beginner to intermediate trails on the Spruce side of the mountain.

Those visitors looking for an adventure with slightly less of an incline can enjoy cross-country skiing, or Nordic skiing, through backcountry terrain. The diverse and vast Nordic trail system crisscrossing Stowe has put the town on the map for cross-country enthusiasts with 30 miles of groomed trails and 19 miles of backcountry terrain. Alternatively, take a snowshoe hike at Smugglers' Notch, which was a passageway for smugglers transporting illegal or embargoed goods across the Canadian border in the early 1800s.

For an après-ski experience, head to one of the many excellent restaurants at Stowe Mountain

Stowe Mountain Resort boasts 116 ski trails and 12 lifts across 485 acres of skiable terrain.

ADVENTURE ALONG THE WAY

BEN & JERRY'S

The Ben & Jerry's factory in Waterbury (15 minutes south of Stowe) churns out more than 350,000 pints of ice cream each year. Tickets for a factory tour are available two weeks out and can sell out quick—but this is a worthwhile stop on any road trip through Vermont. Samples are passed out at the end of every tour, and you can visit the on-site Scoop Shop to discover your new favorite flavor. Guests are encouraged to pay their respects to the "dearly de-pinted" in the Flavor Graveyard—a playful homage to discontinued flavors.

Feast your eyes on Lake Champlain Chocolates' impressive truffle case.

Resort. Try Alpine Hall, an artisanal farm-to-table offering an après menu with cozy dishes like curried pumpkin soup and bites such as fried chicken wings in a maple buffalo sauce. Or embrace the chalet atmosphere at the WhistlePig Pavilion with a fire-baked raclette and whiskey cocktail off its deep and varied drinks menu.

Head into downtown Stowe to check out the Vermont Ski and Snowboard Museum any time of year. The exhibits showcase more than 10,000 items—from equipment and gear to art—that highlight the evolution of snow sports. A few blocks down Main Street rises the picturesque white steeple of Stowe Community Church, one of the oldest nondenominational churches in the United States. Eclectic shops fill the rest of town. Find vintage-style pendant flags at Tangerine and Olive, handcrafted gourmet truffles at Lake Champlain Chocolates, and local fiction at Bear Pond Books in the historic red Depot Building. And for more Vermont dairy, check out Swiss Fondue by Heinz off Main Street for (you guessed it) decadent fondue.

The scenic landscape of Stowe transforms for various events and festivals throughout the year: Watch colorful hot-air balloons fill the skies during the Stowe Balloon Festival in July. Experience a quintessential New England fall while celebrating local artisans during the Stowe Foliage Arts Festival in October. Or join the five-day ski-and-boarding-filled Winter Pride Festival (aka Winter Rendezvous) in January.

OPPOSITE TOP: The von Trapp Family Lodge offers a luxurious resort experience. OPPOSITE BOTTOM: Climb Mount Mansfield for stunning views of the valley. LEFT: Look to the skies at the Stoweflake Hot Air Balloon Invitational (seen here) or the Stowe Balloon Festival.

Just outside town, tucked among rolling hills, green meadows, and thick trees, is the von Trapp Family Lodge, a 2,600-acre mountain resort. The von Trapp family, originally from Austria and the inspiration for *The Sound of Music,* settled in Stowe in the 1940s. The mountain vistas were reminiscent of their home in Salzburg. Opened in 1950 and still a von Trapp family-owned property, the picture-perfect lodge has Austrian-inspired architecture and incredible views. Scottish Highland cows graze in pastures along the hillside, and Katahdin sheep roam the property looking for treats and pets from guests. Enjoy a crisp Austrian-style lager in the rustic wood-clad von Trapp Brewing Bierhall on the resort grounds.

TASTE OF THE REGION

APPLE CIDER DOUGHNUTS

What makes an apple cider doughnut taste so much better than a regular doughnut? These delectable cake doughnuts are spiced with cinnamon, nutmeg, and real apple cider, then rolled in cinnamon sugar and fried to perfection. They are the embodiment of fall flavor. Ideally, apple cider doughnuts are served hot and fresh from a local apple orchard, but Vermonters are also known to bake them at home.

WOODSTOCK

VERMONT

Come fall, Woodstock offers all the classics of Vermont: maple farms, apple cider doughnuts, pumpkin-strewn doorsteps, and the most electric foliage imaginable. It's hard to overstate the incredible vibrancy of the orange, yellow, and red trees along the Ascutney Loop, a popular scenic drive showcasing the New England landscape around Woodstock. In the town itself, you'll find boutiques, galleries, and coffee shops along Elm and Central Streets and hidden gems tucked down alleyways and in 1800s-era buildings. One such gem is Au Comptoir, a magical cocktail bar housed in a white clapboard cottage on Mechanic Street, situated along babbling Kedron Brook. Enjoy seasonal curated cocktails and small bites, or sign up for a private mixology class.

Woodstock's historical legacy is worth exploring between drinks and sightseeing. The town's three founders—George Perkins Marsh, Frederick Billings, and Laurance Spelman Rockefeller—had a profound impact on not just their community but the rest of the United States. It's impossible to imagine it today, but in the 1850s, about 60 percent of the trees in Vermont had been cut down, leaving the land prone to floods and mudslides. But Marsh, Billings, and Rockefeller championed environmental conservationism. Together, they revitalized the region and broadened their advocacy to help create the United States' National Park System. The resplendent foliage that is synonymous with modern-day Vermont represents the founders' legacy and their impact on natural preservation in the United States at large.

You can visit Marsh-Billings-Rockefeller National Historical Park while touring Woodstock. The park's Billings Farm and Museum is a working farm most known for its award-winning Jersey dairy cows and its restored 1890 farm manager's house, which has indoor plumbing, gas lighting, and central heat, considered state of the art in its time. The building, which can be explored on a guided tour, also housed the farm's creamery. Don't skip out on the fresh apple cider and doughnuts in the gift shop, and take an extra moment to meet the newborn calves in the dairy barn.

Like many Vermont destinations, Woodstock is gorgeous in the fall.

PART TWO

SOUTHEAST

Stunning live oaks shade residential Prince Street in Georgetown, South Carolina (page 170).

FAIRHOPE

ALABAMA

Rising from the bluffs over Mobile Bay, Fairhope's beachfront park and quarter-mile-long pier are pristine spots to watch the sunset. The town's charming streets are flanked by colorful azaleas, roses, hydrangeas, and crepe myrtles, as well as live oaks. Mosey down to Fairhope Pier, the "town square" and around the wrought-iron-clad French Quarter to explore this laid-back coastal haven.

Founded in 1894 as a single tax colony by followers of economist Henry George, Fairhope has morphed into a retreat for writers and intellectuals, heavily influenced by the progressive ideas and creativity on which it was founded. Page and Palette, a family-owned bookstore and landmark, epitomizes modern Fairhope, with a rich tradition of readings and other literary events.

Biking trails wind along the coast and through historic neighborhoods. Places like the Grand Hotel Golf Resort and Spa have bikes available to help you explore the area. Built in 1847, the Grand served as a Civil War–era hospital and later hosted training operations during World War II. It has since welcomed presidents, world leaders, and celebrities.

Seafood is synonymous with Fairhope thanks to a jubilee, a natural phenomenon that occurs every summer in the bay. The perfect combination of conditions produces easy fishing for flounder, shrimp, and blue crab. The shrimp stack at the Wash House, the Gulf snapper throats at Sunset Pointe, and the gumbo at Bluegill Restaurant are all delicious local options.

Bucky's Lounge at the Grand Hotel hosts bayview firepits where guests can relax, sip cocktails, and take in the water.

ADVENTURE ALONG THE WAY

MOBILE-TENSAW DELTA

A paddle along the Bartram Canoe Trail will take adventurers through endless hardwoods, tupelo swamps, bogs, and marshes in the Mobile-Tensaw Delta, the largest river delta and wetland in Alabama. Considered one of the most eco-diverse terrains in the country, it is home to bald eagles, kingfishers, egrets, herons, turtles, and alligators. Floating camping platforms allow for multiday trips, a true delight for nature lovers.

GUNTERSVILLE

ALABAMA

Guntersville, Alabama, sits on a hilly peninsula surrounded by its namesake lake, one of the top freshwater fishing lakes in the world. Largemouth bass, striped bass, catfish, and black crappies entice anglers from all over the country to spend a day or two on Lake Guntersville. (Going for the big one? The lake's record weight for largemouth bass is 14.5 pounds.) The town is surrounded by nearly one thousand miles of shoreline and the Appalachian Mountain foothills, prompting its self-bequeathed descriptor "where the mountains meet the lake."

In the summertime, the most important decision of the day is when to get in the water. Besides fishing, the lake offers kayaking or canoeing on the open water or among its shady, canopied offshoot creeks. For those looking for an adventure on dry land, hiking and mountain biking trails twist through the wooded acres of Lake Guntersville State Park. Watch for bald eagles: Their nesting population is dramatically increasing in this region thanks to the conservation efforts of northeastern Alabamians.

Along the lakeshore, City Harbor is a commercial hub filled with excellent restaurants and shops, as well as a place to dock your boat after a day on the water. In town along Old Town Street is the Old Town Stock House, an upscale southern restaurant with a seasonal and locally sourced menu. True to its name, it's housed in an old stockroom in its 1901 building. Plus, the establishment makes its own beef and chicken stock in-house, so the name fits in more ways than one. Much of Guntersville's

Fishermen will beat the sunrise to Lake Guntersville for the best chance at a catch.

TALK LIKE A LOCAL

"CATTYWAMPUS"

The term "cattywampus" is used to describe something in disarray or going poorly, or something in a diagonal direction as it relates to a building, a room's decorations, or a person's clothing. A true southerner might say, "Our day has gone all cattywampus with the turn of the weather," or "The post office is cattywampus from the library."

Communal firepits encourage guests to mingle at ReTreet Resort.

downtown is listed on the National Register of Historic Places, including the rough-limestone Guntersville Armory, which now houses the Guntersville Museum. Constructed under the Works Progress Act of 1936 and used as a training facility during World War II, it is an excellent place to dive deeper into the history of the area.

For a stay marked by true southern hospitality, check out Lake Guntersville Bed and Breakfast in the Hooper House, built in 1910. The inn's wraparound porch beckons guests to sip homemade sangria on a wicker rocking chair while appreciating the lakeside view. A more outdoorsy option a bit farther up the lake is ReTreet Resort, which offers tree houses, tiny cottages, and glamping tents. Whiz around the 40-acre property in a golf cart, indulge in a cedar soaking tub at the Tree Spa, and enjoy an evening under the stars around a firepit.

TASTE OF THE REGION

FRIED GREEN TOMATOES

Fried green tomatoes—sliced unripe green tomatoes that have been covered in cornmeal and fried—are found on many southern menus. It was author Fannie Flagg who made the dish synonymous with Alabama with her 1987 novel *Fried Green Tomatoes at the Whistle Stop Cafe*. They can be served any number of ways but are typically offered with a side of rémoulade. For a fun twist, try them topped with pimento cheese and crispy bacon.

EUREKA SPRINGS

ARKANSAS

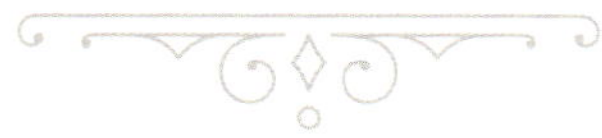

"Curious, indeed" is the motto of Eureka Springs, nicknamed "the town that climbs the mountain." Carved into a mountainside of the Ozarks, this artists' enclave stacks Victorian-era houses and commercial buildings one behind the other on 20 steep hills divided by 19 ravines, with mural-painted staircases connecting one winding bluff to the next.

The Art Colony of Eureka Springs houses two dozen artists in residence, offering a funky, whimsical home for their studios and storefronts. Nearly 15 percent of the town's residents are working artists, and this collective typically adds at least one public art installation to the town each year. "Dogs Walking Hippies," by Doug Myerscough, for example, depicts exactly what the name suggests at Harmon Park, a metal stork perches on Planer Hill, and a seven-foot-tall Big Foot sculpture by Stephen Feilbach crushes a park bench at Lake Leatherwood City Park. Most significantly, the 67-foot-tall modernist ivory statue of Christ of the Ozarks stands high on the grounds of Magnetic Mountain. Art is integral to the atmosphere here.

Eureka Springs has also been a welcoming destination for the LGBTQIA+ community, becoming one of the first in the South to honor same-sex marriages. Find out more about the town's openness to all at the Eureka Springs Historical Museum, named one of the best small-town museums in the United States by *USA Today*. Vintage photographs and local artifacts throughout the museum highlight the town's spirit of inclusion.

Students from Eureka Springs High School collaborated with a muralist on the Rainbow Stairs, one of the most photographed sites in Arkansas.

TASTE OF THE REGION

POSSUM PIE

Possum pie consists of decadent chocolate pudding and cream cheese filling atop a pecan shortbread crust, which "play possum" (a term for pretending to be dead or asleep) under a topping of whipped cream and pecans. Never fear: Possum meat is *not* included.

Theater and music venues abound in Eureka Springs, including the Great Passion Play, which stages the last days of Jesus' life in an outdoor amphitheater.

To see more, hop aboard a green open-air trolley for the Eureka Springs Tram Tour. You'll hear how the discovery of the healing waters of Basin Spring began a boom for the town at the end of the 19th century. Tents became shanties, which became basic wooden structures, which eventually became colorful Italianate, Queen Anne, and Romanesque buildings as visitors flocked to the region for health and rejuvenation. One notable example, Flatiron Flats, forms a V right where Center and Spring Streets split. The entire Eureka Springs Historic District was placed on the National Register of Historic Places in 1970, and there are still more than 60 freshwater springs within the city limits. Lush vegetation, vine-covered grottoes, and historic gazebos mark locations on the Natural Springs Trail, the ultimate walking tour of the most popular springs in town.

Hiking and mountain biking trails crisscross the surrounding landscape, offering fresh-air adventure for outdoorsy folks. For a hike to a panoramic overlook of the verdant Ozarks, venture to the cliff above the White River at Inspiration Point. Lakes, rivers, and springs combine with the mountainside to provide an outdoor haven. Canoe or kayak down Kings River or cruise around Beaver Lake. You can also take in the scenery aboard the Eureka Springs & North Arkansas Railway, which serves lunch and dinner in luxury on a 1940s-era diesel locomotive.

The Great Passion Play Museum and Grounds is a fascinating spot to explore for both religious and

EUREKA SPRINGS & NORTH ARKANSAS RAILWAY
SPRINGS

167
185

OPPOSITE TOP: The Eureka Springs & North Arkansas Railway offers narrated excursions on a seasonal schedule. **OPPOSITE BOTTOM:** Lake Leatherwood City Park is ideal for mountain biking. **LEFT:** Thorncrown Chapel contains more than 6,000 square feet of glass.

---

nonreligious visitors. The 67-foot modernist ivory Christ of the Ozarks statue stands tall on its grounds, and curated features include a Holy Land tour (a replica of East Jerusalem), a collection of religious artwork, and a history museum that explores the Bible's role around the globe. The Passion Play, which depicts the story of Jesus, is performed from May through October. Outside, rugged mountain biking routes attract daredevils from all over the South.

Just outside town, Thorncrown Chapel stands 48 feet tall. The famed church has 425 windows, offering uninterrupted views of its woodland surroundings. This ode to nature's beauty was named a top building of the 20th century by the American Institute of Architects. It's magnificent to behold, well worth a tour, and an ideal place for peaceful reflection.

ADVENTURE ALONG THE WAY

BLANCHARD SPRINGS CAVERNS

Dripping water echoes among the grand chambers of Blanchard Springs Caverns, two and a half hours east of Eureka Springs. The three-level cave system is one of the most spectacular places to explore in Arkansas. Guided tours take visitors past stalactites, stalagmites, and crystalline columns in this continuously changing underground world. Harry Potter fans might think of the underground vaults of Gringotts Wizarding Bank as they wander through chambers—the caverns' lit-up pathways evoke something magical.

AMELIA ISLAND

FLORIDA

Beaches, history, and a ton of charm make up the small town of Amelia Island. Located near the Florida-Georgia border, this is a place vacationers return to year after year.

Upon your arrival, a walk down Centre Street will take you into the historic downtown district, called Fernandina Beach, a 50-block area on the National Register of Historic Places. Cobblestone sidewalks and brightly colored Victorian-era homes are this neighborhood's trademarks. Shrimping boats bob among catamarans in the marina along Front Street, palm trees sway in the ocean breeze, and café lights twinkle at night. The many unique shops and boutiques in Fernandina Beach are worth a browse, including the Salty Local for clothes and the Book Loft for the latest page-turners. Grab a handmade confection at Fantastic Fudge or a locally made brew at the Tavern by Amelia Island Brewing Company (where many of the beers are named after famous women). Visit in May for the island's annual shrimp festival, where the crustacean is celebrated in all manner of dishes, as well as with a parade and decorated shrimping boats. Catch live music and a delicious meal on the patio at the Boat House, or rest and recharge at Elizabeth Pointe Lodge, an idyllic oceanfront inn with white rocking chairs on a wraparound porch overlooking grassy sand dunes.

Amelia Island was first inhabited by the Timucua, a matrilineal Indigenous community of about 30 chiefs and villages. With the arrival of Europeans in 1562 came the unfolding of written history under eight different national flags, which is how this small

Fernandina Beach on Amelia Island offers a historic downtown cityscape.

TASTE OF THE REGION

KEY LIME PIE

Key lime pie is the official state pie of Florida. Sweet and tart, the pie celebrates a Florida crop of old and the state's tropical archipelago. Made with lime juice, egg yolks, and sweetened condensed milk, and often cooked in a graham cracker crust and topped with meringue or whipped cream, the dessert is the perfect tangy summer treat.

Hike, bike, or rest in a hammock at Fort Clinch State Park, where you can also tour the namesake 19th-century fort.

town got the moniker Isle of Eight Flags. First was the French flag, with the arrival of naval officer and colonizer Jean Ribault. Spanish forces drove off the French in 1565, and the red-and-white Spanish flag flew above the island until 1763, when British raids forced out the Spanish. In 1783, the Second Treaty of Paris was signed, returning Florida to Spain. The fourth flag flew when a group of insurgents known as the Patriots of Amelia Island took over in 1812. The fifth flag, the Green Cross of Florida, flew for four months in 1817, coming down quickly when pirates claimed the island on behalf of the republic of Mexico. The flag of the Confederate Army flew for just a year in 1861, until the eighth and final flag—that of the United States—rose over the region in 1862.

There's a whole lot of nature here, too. A canopy of live oak trees dripping with Spanish moss lines the road leading into Fort Clinch State Park. Take the turnout to the Willow Pond Nature Trail, a delightful loop filled with saw palmettos, magnolia trees, and Florida wildlife such as alligators, cicadas, and ospreys. Fort Clinch itself is also well worth exploring. It still smells of old gunpowder, worn leather, and the salty sea. The fort was never finished nor used in direct combat; most of what remains today was completed after Union forces seized control of the area from the Confederacy during the Civil War. Walk through brick tunnels leading to bastions at each corner and climb up a spiral staircase for a view of the northern Amelia Island beaches and the

INSPIRATIONAL
MOON

OPPOSITE TOP: The A. L. Lewis Museum at American Beach showcases the area's heritage and history. OPPOSITE BOTTOM: Spot red admiral butterflies among the foliage on Amelia Island. LEFT: The Book Loft regularly hosts indie book signings and launch events.

Cumberland Sound. The sandy dunes of the beach are popular hunting spots for shark teeth, washed ashore from white, tiger, bull, and lemon sharks known to patrol the waters.

Toward the south end of the island is the historic A. L. Lewis Museum at American Beach. Established in 1935 by Florida's first Black millionaire, Abraham Lincoln Lewis, American Beach was a resort-style retreat for African Americans looking to enjoy what Lewis called "recreation and relaxation without humiliation" during the Jim Crow era. For three decades, the oceanfront playground was filled past capacity. In 1964, Hurricane Dora swept through, devastating homes and businesses. In recent years, there's been a revival to preserve this historic site. Visit the museum and Little NaNa, which is the tallest dune in Florida and a protected historical landmark.

ADVENTURE ALONG THE WAY

BONEYARD BEACH

So called for the bleached skeletons of oak trees along the beach, this hidden gem 20 minutes south of Amelia Island represents a wild side of Florida. Stretching for three miles along the Nassau Sound, Boneyard Beach is a favorite among Jacksonville locals. Within the boundaries of Big Talbot Island State Park, its bluffs and dunes create a wondrous atmosphere and showcase the tree-buffering effect caused by the root systems of the oaks.

MOUNT DORA

FLORIDA

Mount Dora, located less than an hour north of Orlando, exudes laid-back Old Florida charm. Several of its buildings were painted pink for the 1981 film *Honky Tonk Freeway,* and many kept the color, helping the town retain an artsy flair to this day.

For a Florida landscape, Mount Dora sits on a relatively high plateau. The real draws here are access to the water and walkability. It's peaceful on the shores of Lake Dora, and wildlife abounds. Herons, turtles, sandhill cranes, and alligators make their homes among the verdant trees and sandy beaches. Walk along the Palm Island Boardwalk for an elevated nature tour over the water, or kayak in Dora Canal, the link between Lake Dora and Lake Eustis. The only inland freshwater lighthouse in Florida stands proudly at the Port of Mount Dora in Grantham Point Park.

The yellow Victorian-era Lakeside Inn, established in 1883, perches on the shore of Lake Dora and offers delicious dining options and exceptional sunset views over the water. In the historic downtown, independently owned antique shops, local galleries, and outdoor cafés are a highlight. The monthly wine walk, starting at Maggie's Attic and winding through town, is a noteworthy event that brings out locals and visitors alike. Mount Dora is known as Festival City, and its events calendar is booked with fun happenings including the Scottish Highland Festival in February, the Sailboat Regatta in April, and the Craft Fair in October.

Along with its festivals, Mount Dora offers a tasty food scene. Book a dinner at the Goblin Market, where you can sample crab bisque, honey-lavender duck breast, or Yorkshire pudding—among other delicious options—in one of three book-lined dining rooms. Or head to Allyson A Bakeshop for a sweet treat, whether you're craving chocolate brownies, cupcakes, or scones. Meanwhile, Fifth Avenue Streatery offers a fresh take on down-home cooking with a dinner menu that features four different styles of hot dog and six burgers, including the Crabby Burger, with a jumbo lump crabmeat patty.

Visit the lighthouse at Grantham Point on the shores of Lake Dora for a beautiful photo op.

Research
Library

ST. AUGUSTINE

FLORIDA

History and culture meld together where the Matanzas River empties into the Atlantic. St. Augustine, founded in 1565, is the oldest continuously occupied settlement in the United States, and there's a story around every corner. Castillo de San Marcos National Monument, a 17th-century coquina stone fort, is the predominant landmark and history keeper of the area. The fort never saw battle but did change hands four times—from Spanish to English, back to Spanish, to the Confederacy, and eventually to the Union. Each of these historical periods influenced the cultural makeup of St. Augustine at large. Immerse yourself in this history by lodging across from the fort at the boutique St. George Inn, which is within walking distance of several cultural sites and the Floridian, a favorite bungalow-style restaurant. Hop on a trolley tour for a more extensive look at all of St. Augustine's history.

St. Augustine features a rich blend of Gilded Age and Spanish-Moorish architectural styles.

The Historic Colonial District was dictated by the Law of the Indies, a collection of Spanish laws that set the guidelines for city planning. As a result, this area of town matches the historic downtowns of San Juan, Puerto Rico. Coquina stone buildings line the cobblestone streets, which flow from the Plaza de la Constitución, the elongated-obelisk town center used for markets and concerts. Down Aviles Street, the oldest street in the United States, you'll find the St. Augustine arts district alive with brightly painted buildings and tile murals—here, dancing in the street is encouraged. North of the Plaza is Flagler College, part of which is housed in the Hotel Ponce

TASTE OF THE REGION

CONCH FRITTERS

A delicacy of the Caribbean and staple of Cajun cuisine, conch fritters are found on many menus throughout the state—in fact, they're often called the "escargot of Florida." These bite-size deep-fried sea snails are served with a savory rémoulade dipping sauce or mustard aioli.

Tour Castillo de San Marcos National Monument, on the Matanzas River, to see the oldest masonry fort in the United States.

de Leon, a Gilded Age luxury hotel built by railroad magnate Henry Flagler. Believe it or not, these are college dorm rooms—can you imagine? Nearby is another Gilded Age wonder, the Lightner Museum in the former Hotel Alcazar, which was built in the Spanish Renaissance Revival style. In addition to touring the series of rotating and permanent exhibitions, visitors can also rent out venue spaces, including the former casino, once the site of the world's largest indoor swimming pool.

To get a sample of the bohemian local atmosphere, drive north to Uptown for fantastic cafés, shops, and antique stores that line San Marco Avenue. Sunday Gathering Table is a beloved restaurant, with light-filled sunrooms, a delicious brunch, and beach cruisers for rent in the courtyard. The studio of artist Jenna Alexander sits behind the restaurant, which displays her art on its walls, capturing the unique history and laid-back feel of North Florida.

Across the Matanzas River is Anastasia State Park, a stunning haven for campers, beachgoers, and wildlife. Brackish marshes, maritime hammocks, and white sandy beaches make up the landscape, and roseate spoonbills wade in the Salt Run lagoon while ospreys soar the skies. Fort Mose (pronounced moh-ZAY), the first legally sanctioned free Black town in the United States, sits on a beautiful landscape just north of town and is well worth a visit. Stroll the boardwalk, see the interactive museum, or take a ranger-led tour through the replica wooden fort.

78

DAHLONEGA

GEORGIA

The story goes that in 1828, a farmer by the name of Benjamin Parks stubbed his toe on a strange yellow-colored rock while deer hunting on Cherokee land. Word spread that gold had been discovered in the hills of northern Georgia, and miners descended on the area to make their fortune. Dahlonega was born out of that rush, with settlements and buildings springing up overnight. So much gold, indeed, was coming out of the area that the federal government opened a branch of the U.S. Mint here in 1835; it produced more than six million gold coins at its peak before eventually closing during the Civil War. Georgia gold is thought to be some of the highest quality in the world, with a 98 percent purity rate that easily beats that of California and Colorado gold. This heyday is still evident throughout Dahlonega, and can even be seen sparkling in the bricks that make up the historic Lumpkin County Courthouse, now the Dahlonega Gold Museum. A Gold Fever pass gains admission to the museum, the underground cave tours at Consolidated Mines, and an opportunity to pan for gold and gemstones at Crisson Gold Mine. It's a perfect way for families to spend an afternoon—and you may strike it rich!

Dahlonega is like a Hallmark movie come to life. In fact, two movies for the network have been filmed here, with the iconic town circle and historic buildings serving as a bucolic backdrop for the lighthearted flicks. It's not a surprise: Christmastime is magical in Dahlonega, as the whole town is decked out with lights; wreaths and garland are on every tree, door, and fence; and horse-drawn carriages

You can pan for gold or hold gold nuggets or coins at the Dahlonega Gold Museum.

TALK LIKE A LOCAL

"NUGGETS"

If you are from the hills of northern Georgia, you might affectionately refer to yourself as a "Nugget." The term harks back to the gold rush era of the 1800s, and you're considered an honorary Nugget if you've lived in the region for at least 10 years.

Shop and dine on brick sidewalks around Dahlonega's public square, a hub with more than 100 local businesses and restaurants.

make their way around the town square. Even on a nonholiday weekend, the town is packed with visitors looking to enjoy the local charm.

The tight-knit community is apparent all around. Spirits Tavern, famous for its fried green tomatoes, is the local watering hole, where the bartenders greet regulars by name. Tea Rabbit's creates custom teas for local events, community members, and boutiques—and serves the most decadent hot chocolate imaginable.

Numerous wineries surround the area, offering unique varietals made with the state's native muscadine grape, among others. A favorite is Wolf Mountain Vineyards, which has a wraparound deck overlooking the rolling Georgia hills and is packed with visitors and locals alike. Another hot spot is Frogtown Cellars, nestled next to a picturesque pond.

While there are lovely hotel options in Dahlonega proper, like the historic Smith House, many visitors opt to stay in a tree house nearby instead. Dozens of these unusual accommodations are tucked away in the foothills of the Blue Ridge Mountains, with styles ranging from rustic to luxury. They make for an unforgettable experience and speak to the impressive array of experiences that Dahlonega has to offer.

Stay
HISTORIC
Dahlonega
EST. 1833
3 HOUR
PARKING
8:00 AM
TO
5:00 PM

STILL
J.T.S. BROWN
J.W. Dant
Evan Williams
HENRY McKENNA
HENRY McKENNA SINGLE BARREL
PARKER'S HERITAGE COLLECTION
HEAVEN HILL
Fighting Cock
HEAVEN HILL DISTILLERIES, INC.
BOURBON WHISKEY
SERIAL NO. 5,500,000
O.E.D. NOVEMBER 18, 2008
SOUR MASH
R.C. 53G.
HEAVEN HILL BRANDS
D.S.P. KY-1
C
BOURBON WHISKEY
SERIAL NO. 7,000,000
O.E.D. FEBRUARY 10, 2015
SOUR MASH
R.C. 53G.
The Money End of the Barrel
"Distilled Spirits Plant"
"Charred"
"Distilled 160 Proof"
"Original Entry Date"
"Rated Capacity 50 Gallons"
HEAVEN HILL DISTILLERIES, INC.
D S P - KY - 31
C
D 160 P
BOURBON WHISKEY
SERIAL NO. 4,000,000
O.E.D. JAN 13, 1998
SOUR MASH
R.C. 50G.
HEAVEN HILL DISTILLERIES, INC.
D S P - KY - 31
C
D 160 P
BOURBON WHISKEY
SERIAL NO. 2,500,000
O.E.D. JUNE 18, 1982
SOUR MASH
R.C. 50G.
HEAVEN HILL DISTILLERIES, INC.
D S P - KY - 31
C
D 160 P
BOURBON WHISKEY
SERIAL NO. 250,000
O.E.D. DEC 22, 1949
SOUR MASH
R.C. 50G.

BARDSTOWN

KENTUCKY

Known as the Bourbon Capital of the World, Bardstown, about 45 minutes outside Louisville, oozes southern charm. Surrounding the town are bourbon-industry heavy hitters like Jim Beam, Four Roses, Maker's Mark, Heaven Hill, and Bardstown Bourbon Company. You can tour any of these, but for a craft experience, try female-founded Preservation Distillery. The tasting room and facilities at Preservation are housed in refurbished tobacco barns, and longhorn cattle roam the grounds, fertilizing the corn and barley fields. On a tour, you'll learn about the requirements for bourbon: The mash must be 51 percent corn; it must be distilled at no higher than 160 proof and put into a barrel at no higher than 125 proof; the distilled bourbon must be aged in new charred oak barrels; the bottled spirit must be a minimum of 40 percent alcohol by volume and must not contain any flavoring or coloring; and it must be bottled in the United States.

Heaven Hill Distillery houses three tasting rooms and offers a facility tour for those looking to be immersed in the world of bourbon.

Bardstown itself features a plethora of historic brick buildings, some dating back to the late 1700s, such as the Talbott Tavern. Now a beautiful boutique hotel and restaurant, it has been called the oldest Western stagecoach stop in the United States. Old brick mixes with modern amenities, and in some rooms, old iron safes have been converted into closets. Talbott's historic Bourbon Bar is considered the oldest of its kind in the United States and is a must-try if you're a whiskey connoisseur.

Walk outside and you'll find yourself in the heart of Bardstown, where cobblestone streets lead to Scout and Scholar Brewing Company, Cactus Annie's

TASTE OF THE REGION

SOUTHERN FRIED CHICKEN

Fried chicken is about as southern as it gets, and it's oh so delicious. The Fried Chicken Trail takes diners to the best spots throughout Kentucky. Three places on the trail are in Louisville, just shy of an hour north of Bardstown: Shirley Mae's Café, Chicken King, and Dasha Barbours Southern Bistro.

Spot "Little Nis," a sculpted forest giant by Thomas Dambo, in Bernheim Forest and Arboretum.

boutique, the home-goods store Shaq and Coco, and Bardstown Museum Row, a series of four museums including the largest Civil War museum in the country and a museum dedicated to the contributions of women in the 1800s. Just a short drive away from Museum Row is My Old Kentucky Home State Park, home to an iconic 19th-century federal-style mansion. The property inspired Stephen Foster's ballad "My Old Kentucky Home," and during the summer months Kentucky's longest running musical, *The Stephen Foster Story,* is staged at the park's amphitheater. For a phenomenal dinner experience, cross East Stephen Foster Avenue to Toogie's Table for refined regional dishes; the fried chicken is a true taste of Kentucky, and the brisket hash is an ideal weekend brunch item.

About a half hour from Bardstown is Bernheim Forest and Arboretum, a magical place whose Forest Giant Trail takes visitors on a two-mile loop past three mystical giants crafted from locally sourced recycled wood. There are 40 additional trails throughout the forest, winding past fields, lakes, and native Kentucky trees.

The wonderful mix of bourbon and history makes Bardstown a great destination. Speak to locals, and they'll remark on the hospitality, support, and charm of the community. The passion felt for the town's origins—often shared over sips of bourbon—is notable.

ATING
YEARS
MERS!
of all
struments

BEREA

KENTUCKY

The artsy town of Berea lies in the Bluegrass region of Kentucky, tucked against the Cumberland Plateau of the Appalachian Mountains. Considered a keystone for the folk arts and crafts scenes in the state, Berea is also a Kentucky Tourism designated Trail Town and a home base for outdoor exploration. Long ago, the area was simply called the Glade, as there was no real town among the smattering of farms in the region. But in the 1860s, politician and war general Cassius Marcellus Clay and town founder Rev. John Gregg Fee helped establish the region's first racially integrated university, Berea College. In the ensuing decades, rising interest in the cultures and traditions of Appalachia, and the revitalization of crafts in the United States, helped establish Fireside Industries at Berea College as a center for home goods. Today, Artisan Village in Berea's old town still houses studios, handmade craft stores, and boutique shops. Look for the "Studio Artists at Berea: Artists at Work" signs throughout town, or try your hand at regional craftwork through a local workshop program.

The Pinnacles in Berea College Forest has been recognized as the best hike in Kentucky and offers access to stunning vistas, especially at Indian Fort Lookout. Owsley Fork Reservoir is a great spot to kayak or fish. The naturally green water is surrounded on three sides by mountains, with lush vegetation and yellow buttercup wildflowers blooming in the spring. Grab a meal at the Historic Boone Tavern after spending the day outside. The Boone Tavern hot brown—an open-faced roasted turkey sandwich—is a taste of Kentucky tradition.

Woodworker Warren May has been crafting dulcimers in Berea for more than five decades.

TASTE OF THE REGION

SPOONBREAD

Spoonbread, often described as a cross between cornbread and a soufflé, has both Indigenous and Appalachian roots. Berea has been celebrating the hot and creamy dish with its annual Spoonbread Festival every September since 1997.

HOTEL METROPOLITAN
724
METROPOLITAN
HOTEL

PADUCAH

KENTUCKY

At the confluence of the Ohio and Tennessee Rivers lies Paducah, a riverboat community with strong artistic ties. The town has the distinct honor of being in the UNESCO Creative City Network, representing strongholds of creativity around the world—one of only six towns with this designation in the United States.

Internationally, Paducah is known for craft and folk art, particularly quilting. So it goes without saying that a visit to the town's National Quilt Museum is a must. The museum focuses on the medium of fiber art, displaying some of the most intricate, artistic, and compelling quilts from around the world. The museum also offers regular workshops during which guests can learn about and practice quilting on their own, as well as youth education programs, including Quilt Camp.

Afterward, go to Freight House for dinner. Set in a historic railroad depot, the restaurant serves modern twists on classic Kentucky fare and is helmed by chef Sara Bradley, a finalist on *Top Chef: World All-Stars*. The restaurant's menu changes with the season, but the chef's tasting—a six-course meal with an optional wine pairing—is always on offer. Enjoy dishes like green tomato gazpacho, bologna fried rice, and PB&J sticky ribs, to name a few.

One of the most compelling sites to visit in Paducah is the Hotel Metropolitan. Built in 1908 and owned and operated by an African American woman named Maggie M. Steed, it was a stop on

Tour the historic Hotel Metropolitan, built in 1908, which hosted luminaries such as B. B. King, Louis Armstrong, and Duke Ellington.

TASTE OF THE REGION

HOT BROWN

The hot brown has become a staple of Kentucky. The open-faced sandwich was invented in 1926 at the Brown Hotel in downtown Louisville, three hours northeast of Paducah. Consisting of turkey, tomatoes, and a béchamel-cheese sauce atop a slice of bread and topped with strips of bacon, the dish is placed under a broiler for a crispy, hot, bubbling finish.

Walk Second Street—just a block off the water—for some of downtown Paducah's best shopping and dining options.

the civil rights–era chitlin circuit (a network of venues where Black performers could take the stage and share their music during segregation) and listed in the *Green Book,* a guidebook published between 1936 and 1967 that provided safe recommendations for Black travelers in the United States. The Metropolitan hosted prominent guests like Louis Armstrong, Billie Holiday, Thurgood Marshall, Duke Ellington, and B. B. King and was operational until 1996. Now it serves as an African American heritage museum. Tours are by appointment only and run by a group of female volunteers in the Paducah community. It's an incredible time capsule of what life in the 20th century was like for Black Americans, and the tour itself is impactful, entertaining, and memorable.

Theater plays a large role in the fabric of Paducah, and the Carson Center for the Performing Arts accommodates tech runs for many productions headed for Broadway. It's also the performance home of the Paducah Symphony Orchestra. Additional theater experiences take place throughout town, from the Market House Theatre to the Maiden Alley Cinema. You can shop before a show, or after a weekend matinee, in the boutiques downtown—whose colorful flags signify when the stores are open. Kirchhoff's Bakery and Deli, a fifth-generation family-owned and -operated business established in 1873, is the perfect place to grab a sweet treat (like homemade iced shortbread cookies) or a sandwich,

TATTOOS
ART COLLECTIVE

2ND STREET
DIRECTORY
DOWNTOWN

OPPOSITE TOP: Street vendors dot the parks downtown. **OPPOSITE BOTTOM:** Visit chef Sara Bradley's Freight House for a seasonal southern menu and signature cocktails. **LEFT:** The National Quilt Museum features live demonstrations.

such as a fried green tomato BLT and a grilled ham and brie sandwich on cranberry walnut bread.

Adjacent to the historic downtown area is Lower Town, which was revitalized thanks in part to the Artist Relocation Program, which attracted creatives to the area by offering financial incentives to renovate existing properties or build anew. Its success has led to a resurgence of energy in this historic neighborhood. Lower Town was added to the National Register of Historic Places in 1982, and you can take in its 19th-century architecture while browsing myriad art galleries and shops.

Paducah is sustaining culture, identity, and traditions, with art serving as the gateway to deeper connections around the world. Its vibrant community is passionate about history and preservation. As one local remarked, "You can go to the symphony on Friday night and tend to your chickens on Saturday morning." That's the Paducah way of life.

ADVENTURE ALONG THE WAY

WORLD'S LARGEST QUILTING NEEDLE

It's only fitting that a town that celebrates the art of quilting would also have the world's largest quilting needle. Sculpted by artist Michael Terra in 2023, the 22-foot chrome-plated steel needle and thread symbolize the town's love of the fiber arts and connect Lower Town's arts district to the rest of Paducah.

COVINGTON

LOUISIANA

Stretching 24 miles over Lake Pontchartrain is the Causeway Bridge, the world's largest continuous overwater bridge, connecting New Orleans to the more relaxed town of Covington. Dip out of the Big Easy to kayak along the Bogue Falaya, a bayou running alongside Covington, to beat the summer heat, or enjoy Chillin' at the River concerts under the cover of pecan trees in Bogue Falaya Wayside Park.

In the heart of Covington, vibrant pink crepe myrtles and white magnolia flowers bloom within St. John District. When the town was established in 1813, planners laid out Covington in a grid pattern, with square blocks called ox lots intended for trading goods. Colorful, French Quarter–inspired storefronts now line Columbia Street and Lee Lane, with contemporary art spaces like Marianne Angeli Rodriguez Gallery offering abstracts and the historic H. J. Smith and Sons General Store and Museum displaying and selling a treasure trove of antiques.

The Southern Hotel's paneled sitting room is a quiet retreat for its guests.

A historic tour with Royal Carriages provides a unique way to learn Covington's history.

The Southern Hotel, first opened in 1907, underwent a renovation in 2014. Today, the hotel lobby is affectionately called "Covington's living room" for its inviting atmosphere. Hand-painted murals and luxury furnishings mix with tasteful Mardi Gras Krewe antiques to create a warm, embracing environment. Nearby, enjoy contemporary southern fare in a refurbished 1935 railcar at Lola, where blossoms from a Bradford pear tree and live music create an inviting ambience.

TALK LIKE A LOCAL

"LAISSEZ LES BONS TEMPS ROULER!"

In English, *Laissez les bons temps rouler!* means "Let the good times roll!" This Cajun expression isn't exactly grammatically correct in French, so Louisianians embrace it as a Louisianan French Creole expression. The phonetic pronunciation is "LAY-say lay bon tom roulay," which is shouted throughout New Orleans, especially during Mardi Gras. The proper response? *"Oui, mon cher!*—Yes, my dear!"

NATCHITOCHES

LOUISIANA

Marked by magnolia trees along brick-paved Front Street and classic French Creole-style buildings that exude a New Orleans feel, Natchitoches (pronounced NA-kuh-tish) was originally founded as a French colony. Considered the oldest town in Louisiana, it hosts numerous annual celebrations and is full of entertainment for visitors.

Cane River Lake runs parallel to downtown Natchitoches, and the Beau Jardin riverwalk hosts myriad festivals throughout the year. Labor Day weekend draws crowds for the annual Cane River Zydeco Festival, featuring high-energy musical performances (zydeco is a hybrid of blues and Cajun music), dancing, food, and fun.

For hospitality with a local touch, stay at a bed-and-breakfast in one of Natchitoches's elegant Victorian homes, like the Sweet Cane Inn, or a restored Greek Revival home like the Samuel Guy House. The Steel Magnolia House, used as a set for the eponymous 1989 film, is just steps from downtown.

Journey farther up Cane River Lake to see Melrose Plantation, an important stop on the Louisiana African American Heritage Trail and a national historic landmark. A breeze from the water rustles magnolia leaves and the pale pink blooms of okame cherry trees on the 6.5-acre complex. The descendants of freed enslaved people completed construction of the eight buildings on the property, and Melrose has since become a thriving artists' retreat. The "big house" is a beautifully restored example of raised Creole construction, with twin hexagonal

Beau Jardin, with its beautiful greenery and various water features, rests on the banks of Cane River Lake.

TASTE OF THE REGION

MEAT PIE

The official pie of Louisiana has been eaten as a portable street snack since the late 1700s. These meat pies—a blend of beef and pork mixed with onion, bell pepper, and celery, all browned with Cajun spices, wrapped up in a flaky fried turnover, and served with hot sauce—even have their own event: the annual Natchitoches Meat Pie Festival in September.

Docent Betty Metoyer Roque (left), a direct descendant of Melrose Plantation founder Marie Thérèse Coincoin, conducts a tour in front of a mural by Clementine Hunter.

garçonnières (bachelor apartments) its most distinguishing feature. Perhaps the most noteworthy structure at Melrose is the mushroom-shaped African House (circa 1800–1830), which showcases murals of plantation life by acclaimed folk artist Clementine Hunter. The combination of the Congo-style architecture with the unique perspective paintings is a treasure to behold.

The Saline Bayou Water Trail in Kisatchie National Forest is perfect for outdoorsy visitors. Bald cypress and moss-draped tupelo trees rise above the blue-green bayou, where you can kayak or canoe down the 19-mile paddle trail to see woodpeckers, bald eagles, largemouth bass, and white perch. After a day on the water, stop by Cane River Brewing Company, set in a refurbished cotton gin, for a perfect marriage of the progressive yet historically influenced culture of the town.

TALK LIKE A LOCAL

"GRIS-GRIS"

Worn around the neck or waist, a gris-gris (pronounced gree-gree) is a voodoo good-luck amulet meant to protect the wearer from evil spirits. In Louisiana, voodoo, which some sources trace back to enslaved West Africans, incorporated elements of the local Catholic religion in the late 1700s. Today, it remains a spiritual practice with a connection to nature and ancestors. These talisman dolls can be found in stores throughout the state.

CA 1939
SMOOT'S
GROCERY.com
BLUES
YAMAHA
LOW SOCIETY

NATCHEZ

MISSISSIPPI

Natchez (rhymes with "matches") is the oldest town along the Mississippi River. It's rich in culture and heritage shaped by a melting pot of people of Spanish, French, British, and African descent. While most of Natchez is perched on a bluff overlooking the river, a small cobblestone area known as Natchez Under-the-Hill teems with a raucous, scandalous past. The Under the Hill Saloon, with its dark wood and dusty brick walls, is a great place to start a visit. Walk up the hill and along the Natchez bluff to Smoot's Grocery, a tin-sided shack with vintage murals and turquoise barstools that doubles as a juke joint and music venue. Nearby is arguably the best breakfast spot in town, the Little Easy, which serves croissant beignets and specialty coffee that will help you recover from a late night of dancing.

Everywhere in Natchez pulses with history. A 444-mile scenic route from Natchez to Nashville, called the Natchez Trace Parkway, dates to prehistoric times, when the Indigenous Natchez people established their spiritual center at Emerald Mound. In the early 18th century, the French colonized the area, constructing a fort overlooking the Mississippi River and bringing enslaved Africans of the Bambara people here. Wealth accumulated from river ports and cotton plantations after the American Revolution. Between 1820 and 1860, Natchez was the richest town in the United States per capita, and much of its prosperity was built on enslaved labor. The town doesn't gloss over this dark time in its history. Today, the Forks of the Road National Park Service site and monument

Smoot's Grocery is a restored juke joint on the border of Natchez Bluff Park. Come for drinks, street food, and live music.

TASTE OF THE REGION

SOUL FOOD

Mississippi has some of the best soul food restaurants in the country, but the cuisine, which has its origins in African American culinary traditions, is just as commonly made by home cooks. Throughout the state you'll find spreads of pork, green beans, hush puppies, cornbread, collard greens, okra, fried fish, and biscuits and gravy—the pillars of this comforting cuisine.

The Natchez Balloon Festival occurs every fall in the historic downtown. Live music and local art dot the ground while the balloons float overhead.

memorialize what was once the second largest slave trading market in the country. Natchez has also preserved more than 600 examples of historical architecture from before and during the Civil War.

The premier annual event in town is the Natchez Balloon Festival, held each October, during which hundreds of colorful hot-air balloons float above the Mississippi River. Crowds gather for food, live music, and sightseeing as the beautiful balloons race from the bluff over the water. Rosalie Mansion, one of the most influential examples of Greek architecture in the region, serves as the festival grounds. Many of the mansion's original furnishings and items are on display inside, including the only complete double-parlor furniture set in existence, according to the museum's docents. A 400-year-old oak tree outside the columned front porch welcomes visitors back in time.

For a memorable meal, drive under a light-strewn canopy of oak trees to the Castle Restaurant at Dunleith Historic Inn, housed in a historic 18th-century brick carriage house and stables. The Castle serves elevated southern comfort food, like a decadent dish of New Orleans–style shrimp and sweet-corn grits and a sweet-potato bread pudding. The nearby unfinished Longwood mansion is a poignant reminder of the impact and disruptions of the Civil War. Spanning six stories and 30,000 square feet, it remains in its partially completed state and is open daily for on-the-hour tours.

OCEAN SPRINGS

MISSISSIPPI

Red roosters roam freely around the live-oak-lined streets of downtown Ocean Springs. These unofficial mascots of town have local-celebrity status and are an embodiment of this seaside destination's eclectic, artistic feel. Downtown window-shoppers will also see vibrant murals by acclaimed artist Walter Anderson, from Washington Avenue to the Gulf of Mexico. Stop in the Walter Anderson Museum of Art for more work that immortalizes the South's plants, animals, and coastal landscapes.

Downtown Ocean Springs includes more than 200 independent shops, including Hillyer House's art galleries exhibiting glass-blown jellyfish and Coastal Magpie's maritime antiques. For a bite as you browse, visit a bright turquoise shack called Pop Brothers for artisanal ice pops made with fresh fruit, herbs, and spices (strawberry basil is a favorite). Many restaurants in Ocean Springs serve cuisine with French-, Creole-, and southern-inspired flavors. Aunt Jenny's Catfish Restaurant, housed in an 1850s home under a 500-year-old oak tree, serves up fresh seafood with views of Old Fort Bayou Stream; the Julep Room in the cellar was frequented by the likes of Elvis Presley and Billie Holiday.

Fringed umbrellas and picnic blankets dot the shores of Front Beach near downtown. Cypress and magnolia trees mingle with historic oaks along the 15-mile Live Oaks Bicycle Route, connecting Ocean Springs to the Davis Bayou Area. The impeccably decorated Roost Boutique Hotel, named after the town's roosters, is situated steps from downtown.

The Little Room is the crown jewel of the Walter Anderson Museum of Art. Its floor-to-ceiling murals chronicle the daily transformations of nature.

ADVENTURE ALONG THE WAY

SHIP ISLAND

Blue umbrellas and chairs dot the white sand beaches of Ship Island, a barrier island about 12 miles off the coast of Mississippi. Take a ferry and spend the day exploring old Fort Massachusetts or splashing in the clear waters while seabirds squawk overhead.

BEAUFORT

NORTH CAROLINA

In 1997, a legendary shipwreck was discovered just a mile off the coast of North Carolina, near charming Beaufort (pronounced BOE-furt). *Queen Anne's Revenge,* the infamous flagship vessel of the feared pirate Blackbeard, was submerged in roughly 23 feet of water in the Beaufort Inlet. Lost at sea nearly 300 years prior, the ship brought a resurgence of interest in the legendary captain, as well as the town he had visited and terrorized in the 17th century.

Located along the Crystal Coast region of North Carolina, also known as the Inner Banks, Beaufort stretches toward the Atlantic Ocean and has attracted mariners and fishermen since the late 1600s. In those early days, it was known as Fishtowne, and its maritime history mingled with southern charm to create the inviting atmosphere and popular community by the sea of Beaufort today. History buffs will delight in Beaufort's North Carolina Maritime Museum, where visitors will receive an introduction to the era of North American piracy and see a number of relics from *Queen Anne's Revenge.*

After the museum, Beaumont's 12-block historic district continues the journey back in time. It's filled with perfectly intact architecture from the 18th and 19th centuries, with colorful Queen Anne, authentic Greek Revival, and dramatic Gothic Revival buildings lining the manicured streets. The Old Burying

Tour Beaufort by water via rentable kayaks or a guided cruise on a motorized craft. Dive off the shores of Fort Macon for the chance to see a shipwreck.

TASTE OF THE REGION

CAROLINA-STYLE PULLED PORK

One of the oldest barbecue traditions in the United States is shredded, slow-cooked pork. While different regions across the United States have their own seasonings and methodologies, Carolina-style barbecue uses a tangy vinegar-based sauce during and after cooking. Classically served on a fluffy bun with coleslaw dressed with the same vinegar sauce, Carolina-style pulled pork is mouthwateringly tender with a slight kick from cayenne and black pepper.

The Old Burying Ground houses gravesites that predate the Civil War. Nightly ghost tours are sure to stop here.

Ground is a main stopping point on nightly ghost tours; it is one of the oldest cemeteries in the state and has graves dating to the pre-Civil War era.

Many visitors explore Beaufort by sea. Rent a kayak to paddle through waterways across towns and see many popular landmarks. The Rachel Carson Reserve, reachable only by boat, preserves the rich mixture between the area's freshwater and saltwater ecosystems. Carrot Island is a popular stop to watch wild horses roam the tidal marshes. On shore, hiking loops cross over the western end of Town Marsh. During low tide, explorers can look for—but should not remove—seashells and sand dollars while bird-watching on Bird Shoals. The shores of Fort Macon, built in part to fend off pirate attacks in the early days of the colony, conceal a wreck diver's paradise known as the Graveyard of the Atlantic. Rough waters on this stretch of coastline led to numerous shipwrecks, and what remains of those vessels, ranging from wooden ships to German U-boats, still litters the ocean floor.

Downtown Front Street is a magical place to be at sunset. Boats of all shapes and sizes float in the harbor, and the waterfront boardwalk has myriad restaurants with ocean views. Fishtowne Brew House captures the coastal charisma and is a great spot to enjoy a crisp Net House IPA or other nautical-inspired brews.

HIGHLANDS

NORTH CAROLINA

The beautiful scenery of Nantahala National Forest and the Blue Ridge Mountains serves as the backdrop to Highlands, North Carolina, one of the highest-elevation towns east of the Mississippi River. Less than a three-hour drive north from Atlanta and about three and a half hours from Charlotte, Highlands is a weekend getaway for both Georgia and North Carolina residents.

The Highlands area is considered a rainforest, one of only a few in the United States. The mist and rainfall in this region encourage moss to grow on the rocks and trees, giving it a bucolic, almost English-countryside feel. Hike to one of the many waterfalls nearby: Dry Falls offers a walking path that leads directly behind a roaring 75-foot-tall cascade. (The "dry" part of its name comes from the fact that visitors can stand behind the falls without getting wet.) A bit farther from Highlands, find the impressive Whitewater Falls in Nantahala National Forest; this is the tallest waterfall in the eastern United States, dropping more than 400 feet in a series of cascades. The abundant rivers and lakes in the area, including the Chattooga National Wild and Scenic River, provide excellent fishing opportunities for rainbow, brown, and brook trout, as well as largemouth and striped bass. (A fishing license is required.)

Whitewater Falls is the centerpiece of Nantahala National Forest. This is the highest waterfall east of the Rocky Mountains.

ADVENTURE ALONG THE WAY

THE BLOWING ROCK

Three hours north of Highlands, the Blowing Rock, a 250-million-year-old cliff formation in the Blue Ridge Mountains, is steeped in Native American lore. It is said that the Great Spirit answered a maiden's prayer by causing gusting winds to bring her fallen lover back onto the rock. The scientific explanation for this seemingly unnatural wind is the flume formed by the rocky walls of the gorge, through which a northwest wind sweeps with such force that it can actually return light objects tossed over the chasm. A hike to the top of the Blowing Rock is legendary in its own right, with stunning views of North Carolina forests and the Johns River Gorge.

Skyline Lodge places you in the heart of the Great Smoky Mountains. Head to Pinky Falls on a short hike directly from the lodge. A beach and swimming hole await.

One of the first landmarks you'll see in Highlands proper is perched on a hill overlooking Franklin Road, the town's main thoroughfare. The Highlander Mountain House and its accompanying tavern, the Ruffed Grouse, were built in 1885. You can grab a hot toddy by one of the tavern's large fireplaces, surrounded by decor that nods to the area's rich and varied cultural heritage—from the Cherokee nations to homesteaders from Scotland to the moonshiners of the Appalachians. Nearby is the Old Edwards Inn and Spa, built in 1878 as the town's first boardinghouse. It speaks to the original vision of Highlands as a place of retreat and relaxation. Wood-paneled rooms, crackling fireplaces, and stuffed lounge chairs are found throughout the inn. It's a treat to eat at Madison's or the Wine Garden to experience true southern hospitality.

A short drive out of town is Skyline Lodge, a mountaintop hotel designed by Arthur Kelsey. A mentee of Frank Lloyd Wright, Kelsey followed the great architect's ethos of enmeshing a building in its natural environment. Wright's ideology is immediately apparent from the moment you turn onto Skyline Lodge Road and wind up the hillside to the lodge, where a suite is named in his honor. Time your stay around one of the lodge's signature events, including live music nights and its Under the Stars guest chef series. For those looking to take advantage of outdoor adventures in the Great Smoky Mountains, Skyline makes the perfect home base.

OPPOSITE TOP: Downtown Highlands is a noted shoppers' paradise, where antique stores and art galleries abound. OPPOSITE BOTTOM: The Old Edwards Inn and Spa includes a fireside lounge. LEFT: Be on the lookout for northern cardinals while hiking.

There isn't a bad time of year to visit Highlands. During the summer, temperatures rise only to the high 70s, and winter is barely cold enough to see frost on the ground. Red cardinals flit through the trees year-round. A sighting of a northern cardinal's distinctive red plumage is said to evoke spiritual feelings and is considered by some to be a sign from a loved one who has passed.

Overall, this is a place of rest and respite. Stroll down Franklin Road to explore boutiques, stop by Calders Coffee Cafe for a latte, eat a gourmet snack at Edelweiss Pastry Boutique, pop into Dutchman's for home goods, and browse Annawear for unique fashion finds. To find hidden treasures off the beaten path, drive to Reclamations, a sprawling antique warehouse in an old wooden barn.

TASTE OF THE REGION

SWEET TEA

There are few things as classically southern as sweet tea, ideally served ice cold in a mason jar with a wedge of lemon. Sometimes called the "table wine of the South," sweet tea is on offer at virtually all restaurants in the South, and many homes keep a freshly brewed pitcher in the fridge. A note on manners: Simply order "iced tea" to receive sweet tea by default. You must specify if you prefer unsweetened tea, though it might come with an incredulous look upon request—bless your heart.

STOP
S-7-62
CRAVEN S

BEAUFORT

SOUTH CAROLINA

Along a protected intracoastal waterway and about halfway between Charleston and Savannah, you'll find Beaufort, often referred to as the Queen of the Sea Islands. Marshlands, waterways, and a forest of ancient live oaks create the landscape of Beaufort, where you can sit a spell on a cypress tree–shaded bench, catch a lazy breeze off the Beaufort River, and contemplate if life really *is* like a box of chocolates. Though *Forrest Gump* was set in a fictional Alabama town, the beloved 1994 classic was largely filmed in and around Beaufort. That pivotal chocolate-box scene (filmed in nearby Savannah) was shot with confections made at a local shop. The heart of this idyllic town beats around Bay Street, with picturesque shops and cafés along brick-paved streets. Grab a sweet-tea float—two scoops of sorbet topped with southern sweet tea—from Scout Southern Market to immediately put yourself in the Beaufort spirit.

Narrated carriage rides offer old-fashioned tours of Beaufort's downtown area.

Beaufort's historic Craven Street leads visitors to the Point, one of the most iconic neighborhoods in the South. Moss-covered trees frame classic antebellum mansions with deep porches, originally the summer homes of wealthy plantation owners looking to escape the buggy marshland. Many of these residences served as Union hospitals during the Civil War, particularly when Gen. William T. Sherman's advancing army overtook the city, causing Confederate sympathizers to flee. Newly freed

TALK LIKE A LOCAL

"KUMBAYA"

"Kumbaya," or "Come By Here," is a Gullah Geechee spiritual song and, as of 2017, the official State Historical Song of Georgia. The song, which is a plea for better days ahead, was first recorded by descendants of enslaved peoples in the early 1920s. It went on to be recorded by top artists from Pete Seeger to Raffi between 1950 and the 1990s, when it gained a reputation as a campfire song, obscuring its African American origins.

This area is home to rich Gullah Geechee traditions. Here, a master sweetgrass basket weaver creates a new work.

enslaved people were hired to work in the hospitals, and many of them purchased the slaveholders' homes. The Point stands today as a reminder of the multilayered history of the region. Take a carriage tour of the neighborhood and book a room at the Anchorage 1770—a waterfront inn with a worthwhile restaurant and a rooftop bar—to immerse yourself in that history.

Come to Beaufort on a festival weekend for unique sights, tastes, and atmosphere. The Original Gullah Festival celebrates the Gullah people, populations originally from West and Central Africa who were later enslaved in this region. The Gullah Geechee community continues traditions of storytelling, cuisine, music, farming, and fishing, and these take center stage in Beaufort during a Memorial Day weekend event. The Penn Center National Historic Landmark District, across the Woods Memorial Bridge on nearby St. Helena Island, is the former campus of one of the first schools for freed laborers. The vibrancy and remarkable endurance of the Gullah Geechee culture is showcased here, with sweetgrass basketmaking demonstrations, exhibits on the Gullah Fa' Oonah language, and workshops on indigo batik dyeing. Other Beaufort festivals include the annual Beaufort Oyster Festival, held in January; the Beaufort International Film Festival, held in February; the Music Festival of the Lowcountry, held in June; and the Beaufort Shrimp Festival, held in October.

OPPOSITE TOP: Hunting Island allows guests to fish, go boating, or camp at more than 100 sites around the island. **OPPOSITE BOTTOM:** Henry C. Chambers Waterfront Park is a great place to cast off your kayak. **LEFT:** The Ribaut Social Club, located in the Anchorage 1770 inn, offers fine-dining seafood dishes.

Outdoor lovers should visit Hunting Island State Park to see magnolia trees and saw palmettos interwoven with wax myrtles and pines across 5,000 pristine acres. Bike or hike along the Lagoon Trail for peeks of the ocean through the maritime forest. For a panoramic view, climb the 167 wrought-iron steps to the observation deck of the black-and-white Hunting Island Lighthouse. On your way, be sure to stop for shrimp burgers and hush puppies at the Shrimp Shack, the ultimate beach-day spread. Or to the south of Beaufort, walk the wooden boardwalk at Port Royal Cypress Wetlands and Rookery for glimpses of snowy egrets, turtles, and alligators. Golden-hour sunsets bathe Beaufort in a hazy orange hue, creating a romantic setting.

TASTE OF THE REGION

FROGMORE STEW

First, there are no frogs in this recipe! Named for the Frogmore community of St. Helena Island, this stew (also known as low country boil) has four basic ingredients: shrimp, corn on the cob, smoked sausage, and potato, which are often punched up with hot sauce, beer, and seafood seasoning. Traditionally served family style atop newspaper-covered tables, this boil brings people together for a laid-back meal.

Prehistory

GEORGETOWN

SOUTH CAROLINA

The colorful shops and aged brick buildings on Georgetown's Front Street offer a scenic and warm welcome to this South Carolina town. Wave to the residents enjoying sweet tea from their front-porch rockers and take a seat yourself for spectacular views of Winyah Bay and the Harborwalk. Georgetown's welcoming atmosphere can be felt everywhere you go, whether it's Indigo Mercantile for gourmet snacks, Rice Birds for locally made home goods, or River Room Restaurant for seafood with dockside views. This is a small town with a lot of pride.

Georgetown's history can be told largely through two crops: indigo and Carolina gold rice. After the Revolutionary War, the region's murky cypress swamps were transformed into flourishing fields through the work of enslaved West Africans. Because of their labor, by the 1840s, the county had become the wealthiest per capita in the colonies, exporting more rice than anywhere else in the world. Although the rice trade collapsed with the end of slavery following the Civil War—as well as a series of hurricanes that swept through the region in the 1800s—the staple crop's influence on Georgetown remains undeniable. The Rice Museum, under the iconic clock tower in the heart of town, tells the story of that connection, as does the Gullah Museum, which displays crafts and West African artifacts highlighting the fusion of Gullah and southern cultures.

Wildlife enthusiasts will have as much to do in Georgetown as history buffs. More than 200 species of birds, a large population of nesting sea turtles, and the occasional alligator can be spotted at the nearby Tom Yawkey Wildlife Center. The 24,000-acre property was donated to the state of South Carolina by conservationist and former Boston Red Sox owner Tom Yawkey as a wildlife refuge in 1977. Its marshes, wetlands, beaches, and forests spectacularly highlight the natural beauty of the South. Set out on a day hike, or plan ahead to snag a spot on a guided tour—the popular ones tend to book up months in advance.

The Rice Museum presents a history of local agriculture in a 19th-century space.

ARTIN STORYTELLING HALL

JONESBOROUGH

TENNESSEE

In the heart of the southern Appalachian Mountains toward the North Carolina border, Jonesborough is considered Tennessee's oldest town. Established in 1779, predating Tennessee statehood by 17 years, Jonesborough was actually in the unrecognized U.S. state of Franklin before being split between North Carolina and Tennessee when the latter became a state in 1796. Still, many goods made locally in Jonesborough still claim to be from "the lost state of Franklin." You can experience this unusual heritage through historic walking tours, which start at the Chester Inn State Historic Site and Museum and explore tree-lined Main Street and the historic district. Guides dressed in late 19th- and early 20th-century-style clothing point out the intricate federal, Victorian, Greek Revival, Italianate, and Craftsman buildings in town.

Jonesborough has a proud history of acceptance and inclusivity. Forty-five years before slavery was outlawed in the United States, Jonesborough published abolitionist periodicals including *The Manumission Intelligencer* and *The Emancipator*. In the mid-19th century, Jonesborough was also a haven for Jewish immigrants who faced discrimination in other parts of the country.

Today, Jonesborough's history mixes with the eclectic spirit in its various shops and restaurants. Boone Street Market exclusively sells groceries produced within 100 miles of Jonesborough, and the Mill Spring Makers Market features goods from more than 80 local artists and craftspeople. The annual Made Around Here Market in November

Relax in the Wine and Beer Garden at the International Storytelling Festival.

TASTE OF THE REGION

CATHEAD BISCUIT

These large drop biscuits are the size and general shape of a cat's head (if you squint your eyes a bit). Not meant to be fancy, these homestyle buttermilk biscuits are often served with a drizzle of honey and a pat of butter. For a delicious and traditional Appalachian Mountains breakfast, smother them with gravy.

Jonesborough's Main Street includes a historic district that's among the oldest in the United States. The town was founded in 1779, predating Tennessee's statehood.

draws crowds from all over for its wares from regional makers, along with live music and tasty food trucks. Many modern local businesses reside in historical buildings, such as the Tennessee Hills Distillery, in the redbrick former salt house, and Main Street Cafe, housed in the 1930s-era former post office.

Every October, thousands of folks flock to Jonesborough to be moved by personal, soul-stirring tales at the National Storytelling Festival. The festival informally began in 1973, when local journalism teacher Jimmy Neil Smith stood atop a wagon outside the town courthouse and asked residents to tell stories. The festival has become the preeminent event put on by the town's International Storytelling Center, which has helped ignite positive change in the world through connection and empathy.

ADVENTURE ALONG THE WAY

CADES COVE

In Great Smoky Mountains National Park, approximately 70 miles from Jonesborough, is the lush green valley called Cades Cove. An 11-mile loop takes motorists through the popular valley, where they can frequently spot white-tailed deer, black bears, coyotes, and turkeys. Trails crisscross the valley, taking day hikers past restored churches, gristmills, and log cabins left by settlers who cleared the land for farming in the early 1800s. Abrams Falls is one of the most popular hikes and culminates in a rushing 25-foot cascade named after a Cherokee chief who lived in a village downstream.

MIDDLEBURG

VIRGINIA

This quaint town about an hour outside Washington, D.C., is known as America's horse and hunt capital. Middleburg has welcomed equestrians and foxhunters since the early 1900s, and visitors can tour the National Sporting Library and Museum to celebrate and understand that history. (In Middleburg, "sporting" refers to hobbies like hunting and steeplechasing.) Attend the annual springtime Middleburg Hunt Point-to-Point for a steeplechase set in the beautiful Virginia countryside. Look for members of the Middleburg Hunt in their scarlet jackets with apple green collars and brass buttons. They celebrate the sport of foxhunting with a jovial pack of hounds and events throughout the year that dates back to 1728. Attend riding clinics and trail rides in the summer or the annual puppy auction in fall.

The 19th-century center of Middleburg is only a mile long but packs in historic landmarks, unique antique shops, boutiques, and delicious cuisine. Crème de la Crème and Another Blue Moon are two places to hunt for antique treasures. Brick and Mortar Mercantile sells local Virginia goods and cheeky gifts. Upper Crust welcomes visitors to its bakery with a giant cow statue and is known for its "cow puddle" cookies—a thin and crispy take on a chocolate chip cookie. King Street Oyster Bar, situated in a former bank building, is packed almost every night, for good reason: It serves the freshest oysters in the area.

A brass fox-shaped knocker on a red door greets guests at the Red Fox Inn and Tavern, a landmark in

The Middleburg Hunt, a sporting organization since 1906, meets thrice weekly throughout the fall and winter.

TASTE OF THE REGION

BALLPARK PEANUTS

Grown in southeastern Virginia, about four hours south of Middleburg, since the 1860s, the crunchy ballpark peanut is unmatched in flavor. It's shelled for use in gourmet snacks and peanut butter, and sold whole and hot at baseball games. Most people prefer the ballpark treat roasted and salted, but raw or boiled preparations are just as tasty.

The Red Fox Inn and Tavern offers a four-course menu in its tavern, but you can visit the pub for more casual fare (though caviar flights are still on offer).

the heart of town that dates back to 1728. White roses climb the fieldstone walls in the courtyard gardens, and the inn's brick-laden pathways lead through secret gardens to individual cottages. Tasteful, quintessentially Virginian decor fills the rooms, including playful bronze fox statues and paintings depicting horsemen on the hunt.

You can also book a stay at the Goodstone Inn & Restaurant, set on 265 bucolic acres, with 18 cozy accommodations spread across six guest houses. Enjoy farm-to-table dining, a heated saltwater pool, and peaceful pastimes like kayaking along Goose Creek.

Northern Virginia's Piedmont region has ideal growing conditions to produce the full-bodied Petit Verdot wine grapes, and sprawling vineyards fill the countryside surrounding Middleburg. Green fields and rows of vines lead to the white stone courtyard at Boxwood Winery, which also has the distinction of being one of the earliest and most acclaimed horse farms in the area. A red barn and gazebo sit atop a lovely hill at Cana Vineyards, a female-owned winery known for its award-winning Cabernet Franc Rosé. Surrounded by the Bull Run and Blue Ridge Mountains, it's not difficult to find an idyllic vista to enjoy for an afternoon.

HARPERS FERRY

WEST VIRGINIA

Harpers Ferry might be tiny, but it holds a great amount of significance for the United States. It feels as though time has stood still as you walk along the town's cobblestone streets and among mossy rock walls.

You will find a bit of history around every corner here. Most notably, the Harpers Ferry National Armory and Arsenal guardhouse was the site of John Brown's unsuccessful revolt in 1859. Brown was a staunch abolitionist dedicated to destroying the institution of slavery. While the failed raid led to his death, it helped inflame tensions between the North and South to the point of no return, and it is thought to be a major impetus for the start of the Civil War.

In 1868, three years after the end of the Civil War, Harpers Ferry became the site of Storer College, a historically Black institution open from 1865 to 1955. You can tour the school as well as visit the Underground Railroad sites dotted throughout town. (Harpers Ferry National Historical Park is also part of the National Underground Railroad Network to Freedom, a program that commemorates sites with a verified connection to the Underground Railroad.) The Black Voices Museum is also an excellent stop to learn more about Black history in the area. Exhibits focus on the 200-year fight for equality and freedom from the Civil War to the civil rights movement.

Two bridges cross over the meeting of the Potomac and Shenandoah Rivers into Harpers Ferry—one bridge for people, the other for trains. The Maryland Heights Trail, where you can spot peregrine falcons and bald eagles, has a popular

Hike the Maryland Heights Trail for the best view of Harpers Ferry.

TASTE OF THE REGION

PEPPERONI ROLLS

Originally made as a grab 'n' go lunch for coal miners working underground in the first half of the 20th century, the pepperoni roll is about as classic West Virginia as it gets. This finger food, consisting of a fluffy bread roll stuffed with pepperoni and mozzarella cheese, can be found in restaurants, grocery stores, gas stations, and tailgates throughout the state.

Explore the Victorian buildings, shops, and eateries of downtown Harpers Ferry.

overlook of this intersection and offers views of Lower Town Harpers Ferry. Victorian homes and 150-year-old row buildings with museums, shops, and restaurants make up the town center. Vintage Lady and Tessoterica both specialize in handmade West Virginia goods, and True Treats stocks nostalgic and historic candies, including some made with Civil War–era recipes. From most places in town, you'll be able to see the Victorian Gothic spire of St. Peter's Roman Catholic Church, built in 1833, at the top of a hill.

Less than an hour and a half from Washington, D.C., Harpers Ferry is a popular spot for weekend getaways throughout the year or as a day trip for visitors spending time in the nation's capital. And there are a surprising number of delicious restaurants and beautiful outdoor offerings to enjoy around Harpers Ferry. The Barn of Harpers Ferry, housed in (what else) a big red barn, is where locals go for live music and a cold beer. Fill up on scones and cinnamon buns from Bolivar Bread Bakery before heading out on the portions of the Appalachian Trail that cut directly through town, or to hike on Virginius Island, where you can explore ruins of a gristmill and canal along the Shenandoah River. The Blue Ridge Mountains surround Harpers Ferry on three sides, creating a beautiful oasis of land and water, and floating down the Potomac in a canoe or kayak is the perfect summertime activity.

Studio40
THE BAKERY
130
Studio40
Fine American Crafts
Regional Art
Art to wear
130

LEWISBURG

WEST VIRGINIA

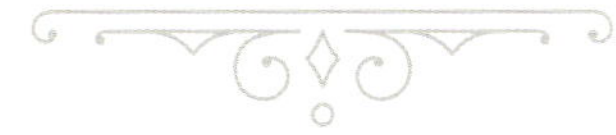

Amid the Allegheny Mountains countryside—with narrow roads winding through idyllic farmlands, shaded ponds hidden by blooming orchards, and the babbling waters of the Greenbriar River—find art, history, and outdoor recreation in Lewisburg.

The past and present exist in harmony throughout town. The 18th- and 19th-century buildings have been converted for new purposes, such as Lee Street Studios, a gallery housed in what was a 1924 elementary school, and Hill and Holler, a rental outfitter, beer bar, and performance venue in the old Fort Savannah Motel. Carnegie Hall, built in 1902, has been offering live performances to more than 75,000 patrons a year since it opened. Especially popular are the Ivy Terrace concerts, performed outside to audiences sprawled out on lawn chairs and picnic blankets. The Greenbrier Valley Theatre Company performs at Carnegie Hall year-round.

The Greenbrier River Trail is a peaceful 78-mile route for hikers, bikers, and horseback riders; it winds along the river and through the countryside. Hiking the Forks of Cranberry Trail in the Cranberry Wildlife Management Area is a popular way to spend a morning, particularly after fueling up with coffee from the Wild Bean.

For a more relaxing day, check out the Historic General Lewis Inn, which has been in continuous use since 1929. The horse-drawn carriage out front gives a nostalgic touch, and the dining room serves contemporary southern cuisine.

Studio 40 on Washington Street features limited-edition clothing, jewelry, and accessories, along with craft glass and ceramic work.

ADVENTURE ALONG THE WAY

LOST WORLD CAVERNS

Descend 120 feet into the earth at Lost World Caverns. Witness the nation's largest compound stalactite, a 30-ton formation called the Snowy Chandelier, and a sparkling white column of calcite called the Bridal Veil. These two rock formations make explorers feel like they're walking a prehistoric planet. The caverns, discovered in 1942, are located on a farm just a few minutes from downtown Lewisburg. Families of all ages will enjoy this adventure below the surface.

PART THREE

SOUTHWEST

Visit Texas Hill Country in spring to see the state's iconic bluebonnet wildflowers.

BISBEE

ARIZONA

From mining town to artistic community, Bisbee, in southwest Arizona, is a colorful shock in the desert thanks to the surrounding orange peaks of the Mule Mountains and the turquoise, red, and yellow Victorian-style storefronts lining the streets. Unlike the typically dry, hot climate Arizona is known for, Bisbee has a temperate climate year-round, even catching a dusting of snow in the winter. Visit anytime of year to explore this funky, culturally rich destination.

The Bisbee Mining and Historical Museum tells how the mines in Mule Mountain were among the richest mineral sites in the world during their heyday in the early 1900s. As the mines prospered, so did the city, and many of the historic buildings of Bisbee seemed to pop up overnight. When the mines closed in the mid-1970s, a rush of hippies and free spirits took up residence to pursue the arts. While the mining history shaped the town, art and music have made Bisbee what it is today.

Vibrant Bisbee nestles right into the slopes of the Mule Mountains. Enjoy a hike before the heat takes over the day.

For a dive into the past, the Queen Mine tour takes visitors 1,500 feet underground in an actual old mining car. Wearing hard hats, miners' headlamps, and yellow slickers, guests get a taste of what life was like deep inside the earth. The Lavender Pit, a former open-pit copper mine, can be appreciated via surrounding viewing decks. This is a great place to spot Bisbee turquoise—also known as Bisbee blue—a high-quality stone found in the area. In the mine's copper-producing days,

TASTE OF THE REGION

NAVAJO FRY BREAD

Fry bread, a puffy, golden-brown, deep-fried disc of dough, is made of simple ingredients: flour, baking powder, lard, salt, and sometimes sugar. Navajo fry bread is a traditional Native American staple that goes back generations. While it has contentious beginnings (it is thought to have originated as a means of survival during marches when Indigenous tribes were forced to relocate from their homelands to reservations), it is often seen as a ubiquitous symbol of Native American resilience.

The Bisbee Art Wall off Brewery Avenue showcases an outdoor display from local artists.

the turquoise was considered valueless. Today, the smoky blue stones are extremely rare and highly prized among collectors.

Downtown, museums and galleries feature everything from local to international works. The Artemizia Foundation's museum houses a permanent collection with pieces by Andy Warhol and Banksy, along with rotating seasonal galleries. Murals and street art are found all over town, and the word "cool" best describes the cafés, thrift shops, and locally owned stores. Óptimo Hatworks crafts elegant, one-of-a-kind hats. Classic Rock Couture is filled with hanging plants and vintage finds such as records and plush orange sofas.

Stay in a restored Airstream or even a 1947 yacht at Shady Dell Vintage Trailer Court for a uniquely Bisbee getaway.

TALK LIKE A LOCAL

"SNOWBIRDS"

Snowbirds migrate in huge numbers to the warm Arizona climate during the winter. No, these aren't actual birds, but rather people seeking warmer weather, typically retirees from northern states. If a snowbird becomes a permanent resident after a warm winter in Arizona, they are then referred to as a sunbird. Some locals don't like the traffic that snowbirds bring to their cities, but the undeniable economic boom might be worth the longer winter commutes.

INMATE HOLDING AREA
SINGLE FILE ONLY
CAMERAS IN USE
OBEY OFFICERS
DANGER
HIGH
VOLTAGE

SILVER CITY

NEW MEXICO

Located in the southwestern corner of New Mexico and surrounded by the Pinos Altos Mountains, this unique high-desert town calls to both outdoorsy and creative types. In downtown Silver City, colorful storefronts line the main drag, Bullard Street. There's a bohemian, artsy, southwestern vibe, with building facades painted in bright turquoise, soft orange, and brilliant magenta. Vibrant murals made by young artists from the Youth Mural Program depict the history and culture of the region and are on display throughout downtown. Every July, the Clay Festival explores and celebrates the medium as an element that unifies New Mexico; acclaimed artists from around the world display thought-provoking pieces and host workshops for people of all ages who want to learn to shape and play with clay.

About 50 miles north of Silver City, explore Gila Cliff Dwellings National Monument in Gila National Forest. Guided tours of the dwellings give hikers a glimpse into the lives and culture of the agricultural Mogollon people, most active in this region from the 1280s through the early 1300s. Deep, colorful, volcanic rock-walled canyons, rolling juniper and upland grasslands, aspen glades, and high desert mesas make up the park, which has a seemingly unlimited number of hiking and backpacking trails. The Gila Wilderness is the nation's first designated wilderness area, meaning the remote landscapes remain completely untouched and natural ecosystems function without permanent improvements or human habitation. Be respectful during a venture here, and observe leave-no-trace principles.

Visit Gila Cliff Dwellings National Monument for breathtaking views of Mogollon rooms from the 13th century.

ADVENTURE ALONG THE WAY

FOUR CORNERS MONUMENT

Make a stop at the only spot in the United States where four states meet. Set foot in New Mexico, Arizona, Colorado, and Utah and have the unique privilege of being in multiple places at once.

TAOS

NEW MEXICO

The blending of Native American, pioneer, and northern Mexican cultures shapes Taos into a quintessential southwestern destination. The high desert offers a beautiful and rugged landscape for this artistic community in northern New Mexico, as well as plenty of unique outdoor opportunities. Taos exudes effortless individualism through the preservation of the region's history and support from local businesses, boutiques, restaurants, and galleries. All buildings within the city limits are constructed with an adobe facade, with wooden beams and turquoise accents peeking through the brown-orange clay.

Taos Pueblo, at the base of the Sangre de Cristo Mountains, is a fascinating place to visit. The series of adobe structures—including a ceremonial site and multistory dwellings—has been continuously inhabited for more than 1,000 years by a thriving community. The Tiwa Puebloans inhabited the area until 1540, when European explorers from the Francisco Vásquez de Coronado expedition found the Indigenous community and their settlement. The land and settlement were returned to the Taos people in 1970, and about 300 modern Puebloans live full-time in Taos Pueblo today. These structures helped inspire the Pueblo Revival style of architecture seen throughout contemporary New Mexico.

Every nook and cranny in historic Taos Plaza is steeped with art and culture. Alleyways off the main plaza are lined with desert marigolds and purple lilacs and lead to hidden gems, such as Lun + Ojo, which carries works from local artists and curated

Attend the annual Taos Pueblo Pow Wow to cheer on participants in the Native American dance competition.

TALK LIKE A LOCAL

"CHRISTMAS"

When ordering tamales, enchiladas, or pork stew, your server will always ask if you want "Christmas," meaning red and green chile sauces, on your meal. The correct answer is always yes. The particular blend of red and green means more complex flavor and just the right amount of heat.

The San Geronimo church was reconstructed in 1850 after the previous church was destroyed by cannon fire during the Mexican-American War.

vintage items. Four miles from downtown, Chimayo Trading Del Norte embodies the arts scene, with its Navajo rugs, Pueblo pottery, and Native American jewelry. As you search for that perfect piece of turquoise jewelry and stumble upon a painting from a native Taoseño, you'll start to understand the town motto: "Taos is art."

While many restaurants in Taos imbue hospitality, none welcomes visitors more than the Love Apple. Housed in an 1800s church once called the Placitas Chapel, it sources nearly every ingredient on the menu locally and sustainably, giving the place a magical sense of home cooking. A whitewashed patio with candles and café lights entices diners to unwind with a memorable meal. The restaurant's menu changes seasonally, based on what local growers can provide. Previous dishes have included buttermilk yellow and blue cornbread, a baked tamale with Oaxacan-style mole, and house-made potato gnocchi served with butternut squash tomato sauce, burrata, and fried sage.

On the last full weekend of October, colorful hot-air balloons fill the skies during the Taos Mountain Balloon Rally. Watch from the ground or take your own ride in the sky, with views of the New Mexico mesas stretching for miles beneath you.

For a different once-in-a-lifetime adventure, whitewater raft through the Rio Grande via the 800-foot chasms of the Rio Grande Gorge, past

REST ROOMS

OPPOSITE TOP: Hike the Rio Grande Gorge at sunset for stunning views of the Sangre de Cristo Mountains. **OPPOSITE BOTTOM:** The John Dunn House Shops host many small businesses downtown. **LEFT:** The Love Apple restaurant crafts seasonal New Mexican cuisine.

ancient petroglyphs and rock formations. Or see the river from a bird's-eye view on the Rio Grande Gorge Bridge, which stands about 565 feet above the river, making it one of the highest bridges in the country. Farther north along the river are the rock-walled pools of Manby Hot Springs. Concentric-circle petroglyphs mark the naturally occurring springs, indicating centuries of human use, but it was a late 19th-century self-proclaimed British entrepreneur and land thief named Arthur Manby who "officially" named them after himself. While Manby was unsuccessful in turning the springs into the world-class resort he dreamed of, they remain today to rejuvenate whoever stumbles upon them. Oh, and one important note: Clothing is optional.

ADVENTURE ALONG THE WAY

SAN FRANCISCO DE ASÍS MISSION CHURCH

Each spring, the *enjarre,* or re-mudding ritual, helps preserve the gorgeous adobe walls of San Francisco de Asís Mission Church, just a few miles from downtown Taos. Here, four white crosses—three above the adobe Spanish colonial beehive buttresses and one above the entryway—soar into the blue desert sky, inspiring the likes of painter Georgia O'Keeffe and photographer Ansel Adams. Constructed between 1772 and 1816, the church is a national historic landmark and an active parish.

BROKEN BOW

OKLAHOMA

A trip to Broken Bow in southeastern Oklahoma offers time to rest and recharge in a natural oasis. Massive shortleaf pine, hickory, and red oak trees tower above the cool, clear waters of Broken Bow Lake. The verdant, hilly forest is a contrast to the rest of the state, where plains and sky stretch as far as the eye can see. To experience the beautiful forested slopes and vistas in the area, take the Talimena National Scenic Byway, which winds through Ouachita National Forest. It'll set the tone for a stay in Broken Bow, where life is all about slowing down and enjoying the great outdoors. Renting a cabin in the woods is the way to go, with options ranging from luxury to rustic. Enjoy a summertime retreat on Broken Bow Lake, whether you choose boating, floating, or swimming.

Broken Bow partners with surrounding towns for beloved annual festivals, like the Twice as Fine Texarkana Wine Festival in May, the Woodturning Competition in September, and the Beavers Bend Annual Folk Festival and Craft Show in November. Fuel up with coffee from Hochatown Trading Post and Coffee Company before the day's adventures begin. And stop by Abendigo's, just north of town, for live music, craft cocktails, and seasonal menus.

Mountain Fork River flows from the base of Broken Bow Lake through Beavers Bend State Park and provides excellent fishing, river floating, and canoeing. In the Forest Heritage Center, large wood-art dioramas depict the history and impact of forests on modern culture, painted by "Smokey Bear" artist Harry Rossoll.

Broken Bow is a great destination for families looking to spend time exploring together. Kids of all ages will love a train ride from the Beavers Bend Depot aboard a replica of the 1863 C.P. Huntington S.P. train engine, a 30-minute jaunt through the woods of Beavers Bend State Park. Or saddle up for a guided horseback trail ride through the park, with a scenic two-and-a-half-mile loop that can be ridden at just the right pace.

Head out early to see the sunrise over the Mountain Fork River in Beavers Bend State Park.

GUTHRIE

OKLAHOMA

A stroll down Division Street in Guthrie transports visitors into an old Western film. Known theatrically as America's back lot, this small town 40 minutes north of Oklahoma City is filled with late 19th- and early 20th-century commercial architecture, making it a popular setting for period films. More than 2,000 buildings can be found in Guthrie's historic district, designated a national historic landmark. Many of these have been retrofitted to house modern business, like Gallery Grazioso in the 1902 brick building formerly occupied by the Pabst Brewing Company. With a mixture of international goods and limited-edition signed prints from musicians and artists, the gallery offers a wonderful representation of the art that brings color and zest to modern Guthrie.

Guthrie is a place for those who aren't in a hurry. Shop owners are easy to chat with and happy to share restaurant recommendations. Try Gage's Steak House, a local favorite in the Old Santa Fe Train Depot. For an active weekend, visit Guthrie during the 89ers Day Celebration in April. The festival remembers the Oklahoma Land Run of 1889, in which the unassigned lands of the government-deemed "Indian territory" (land designated for Native Americans but not assigned to a specific tribe or community) were opened for white settlement. This land run ultimately heralded Oklahoma as the 46th state in 1907. Guthrie sits on much of the original settlements from the Land Run and was Oklahoma's first state capital.

Oklahomans celebrate the Land Run of 1889 with a parade, carnival, and rodeo.

TALK LIKE A LOCAL

"BOOMER"

College football spirit from the nearby University of Oklahoma (OU) can be felt throughout the state. "Boomer" is a commonly shouted greeting to fellow OU fans, and the only reply necessary is "Sooner." The origins of this exchange are questionable (perhaps even derogatory), but the state has embraced the phrase. Now it's heard in megaroars across OU's stadium every time the team scores a touchdown.

FREDERICKSBURG

TEXAS

The best place to sip a crisp German beer in the Southwest is in a small town between San Antonio and Austin called Fredericksburg. Founded by German immigrants in 1846, Fredericksburg embodies a surprising duality between Texan and German cultures. Food and beer in particular are the optimum ways to celebrate the heritage of the region, especially via the farm-to-table duck schnitzel at Otto's and the smooth Kölsch at Altstadt Brewery.

A park called Marktplatz sits in the center of town, where gardens and sculptures lead to the Vereins Kirche Museum on the original site of Fredericksburg's first school and church, built in 1847. Nineteenth-century buildings with casement windows and standing-seam tin roofs line Main Street. On the thoroughfare, you'll find the Pioneer Museum, which tells the story of the German farmers who originally settled the town. Many of these settlers' descendants still live in Fredericksburg.

The Pioneer Museum includes 10 historic structures staged to evoke and educate on the history of Gillespie County.

The Smithsonian-affiliated National Museum of the Pacific War, meanwhile, tells an impactful human story of World War II. Fleet Admiral Chester W. Nimitz grew up in Fredericksburg in the 1880s and '90s, and the museum honors his life and those of the people who served with him. Live demonstrations and reenactments of various battles breathe life into the struggles of the Pacific theater, and the Japanese Garden of Peace allows space for reflection on the war and ongoing relations between Japan and the United States.

ADVENTURE ALONG THE WAY

LUCKENBACH

A 15-minute drive from Fredericksburg takes you to a small trading outpost opened in 1849. Now home to a historic hall used for daily live music and weekend dances, Luckenbach is a gorgeous place to relax under 500-year-old oak trees. The likes of Willie Nelson and Waylon Jennings have performed at Luckenbach, and on Sunday afternoons, informal concerts invite anyone who's willing to play for the crowd.

The National Museum of the Pacific War features the Japanese Garden of Peace, completed in 1976 as a symbol of friendship between Japan and the United States.

Winemakers recently discovered that the climate of Fredericksburg's Gillespie County is ideal for growing grapes. The mineral-rich soil and dry weather have led to a modern explosion of vineyards and wineries, which now make up Wine Road 290. The estate at Augusta Vin is an idyllic setting to enjoy the best of Texas Hill Country wine. The two-story tasting room and elegant courtyards sit among rows of green vines with beautiful views of the property. The Wine Barn at Signor Vineyards features live country music and white Adirondack chairs tucked under oak and pecan trees.

Lush rows of wildflowers grow over hundreds of acres at Wildseed Farms, just minutes from downtown Fredericksburg. Here, Texas bluebonnets, red poppies, and yellow sunflowers stretch toward the sun along walking paths and butterfly gardens. This largest active wildflower farm in the country includes a beer garden, plant nursery, and seed shop where you can purchase native varietals.

Hikers might spot golden-cheeked warblers and black-crested titmice along the treks at Enchanted Rock State Natural Area. The park's namesake, a mystical rocky pink dome formed when liquid magma turned to granite over a billion years ago, rises high above the countryside. Indigenous communities as far back as the Clovis people, who lived in North America some 13,000 years ago, have considered the area sacred ground. Prickly pear cacti and side oats grama grass line the trails to the top

OPPOSITE TOP: Refresh yourself at the Brewbonnet Biergarten after shopping the plants at Wildseed Farms nursery. **OPPOSITE BOTTOM:** Signor Vineyards hosts tastings by reservation, but walk-ins are welcome, too. **LEFT:** Enjoy the bluebonnets at Enchanted Rock State Natural Area.

---

of Enchanted Rock, where views of the hillside are spectacular at sunset. More impressive is the stargazing at night: It is an International Dark Sky Park, ensuring high-quality observation.

To stay immersed in the natural setting of Texas Hill Country, reserve a tree house at Onera, just outside Fredericksburg's downtown. Repurposed shipping containers, geodesic domes, and luxury canvas tents are set in juniper and oak trees, with private soaking tubs and firepits to enjoy under the Texas night sky. Just off Main Street are the colorful cottages of the Trueheart Hotel. Rooms are decorated with a tasteful nod to Texas, a limestone fireplace offers a place to commune over a glass of wine in the evening, and you'll get a morning delivery of hot buttermilk biscuits.

TASTE OF THE REGION

PEACH BUTTER ICE CREAM

Peak peach season is mid-May to mid-August in Texas. Find some of the juiciest at Vogel Orchards, right outside Fredericksburg. The orchard also sells homemade peach products, including a delicious peach butter ice cream that captures the taste of Texas—a creamy and sweet delight with a touch of spice from cinnamon and nutmeg. Nearby Jenschke Orchards is a pick-your-own-peaches spot that also serves homemade ice cream alongside gourmet products.

PRADA
MARFA
PRADA
MARFA
PRADA
PRADA

MARFA

TEXAS

Tucked between the Davis Mountains and Big Bend National Park, Marfa is an artistic paradise in the Chihuahuan Desert.

Originally built in the 1880s as a water stop along the Southern Pacific Railroad, Marfa emerged on the American Southwest art scene when minimalist visionary Donald Judd moved to town and established the Chinati Foundation, a contemporary art museum aimed at preserving permanent large-scale installations. What followed was a flood of world-class artists and galleries. The "Prada Marfa" sculpture, about 40 miles from town, by artists Michael Elmgreen and Ingar Dragset is particularly iconic. For something closer, visit Ballroom Marfa, a 1920s-era ballroom turned free contemporary art museum.

The Sentinel Marfa, a cocktail bar and restaurant set inside an active newspaper office, beckons guests to enjoy locally sourced treats. For an artsy lodging option, the Thunderbird Marfa is a renovated midcentury motel with a center courtyard of desert grasses and honey mesquite trees.

On clear nights, look for the mysterious "Marfa lights," glowing orbs that dance on the horizon on the southeastern edge of town. There are several local interpretations of the phenomenon: Some folks say the orbs are reflections from nearby campfires; adherents of Mexican folklore say they're shape-shifting owls and witches keeping an eye on townsfolk; and others believe they're signs from alien life-forms. Whatever you believe, the lights fittingly play into the intrigue of this remote West Texas town.

"Prada Marfa" is a permanent art installation constructed in 2005. The inaccessible interior still contains goods from Prada's fall/winter collection of that year.

TASTE OF THE REGION

MARFA BURRITO

Marfa Burrito is a hole-in-the-wall that treats customers like family and serves affordable, delicious burritos that actor Matthew McConaughey has regularly praised. The handmade tortillas are massive, the salsas are packed with flavor, and the breakfast burritos are the best way to start the day. This West Texas icon has only a few menu items and a strict cash-only policy.

OCEAN KAYAK

PORT ARANSAS

TEXAS

Just south of Corpus Christi on the Gulf Coast is the beachy town of Port Aransas, or Port A to locals. Before this town existed, locals called the area Tarpon, for the large fish that swim in the nearby waters. Today, Port A is known as the fishing capital of Texas. Charted fishing expeditions offer anglers the chance to reel in redfish, flounder, black drum, or trout, with deeper adventures into the gulf for tuna, kingfish, sailfish, and marlin. The Deep Sea Roundup, the oldest fishing tournament on the Texas coast, attracts competitive fishermen and hobbyists each summer. Of course, the cuisine in town highlights the freshest catches. The mermaid soup at Lisabella's, made with lobster, shrimp, and curry, is legendary, and the Black Marlin Bar and Grille serves award-winning shrimp and grits.

Casual beachgoers in Port A can sit in orange beach chairs under scallop-edged umbrellas at Cinnamon Shore. Beach cottages line the dunes and offer excellent sunrise views over the gulf. This is an excellent place to rent a house for the ultimate summer vacation, with paddleboard yoga, evening beach bonfires, and dune buggies available for a season's worth of fun. Golf carts are the preferred mode of transportation around Port Aransas, and visitors will often see entire families crammed into the tiny vehicles as they zip down the street. Book a stay in April during the highly anticipated Texas SandFest, the largest beach-sand sculpture competition in the country. Artisans create incredibly intricate constructions, and live music fills the salty air.

Redfish call the shallow flats near Port Aransas home. These waters have become popular with fishermen.

TALK LIKE A LOCAL

"COKE"

In Texas, any carbonated soft drink, regardless of flavor or brand, is lumped into one generic term, and that is a "Coke." So, at a restaurant when you tell a server you'd like a Coke, you'll likely be asked what kind. Then it's your turn to specify if you mean a Coca-Cola or another soda.

Visitors can camp right on the beach at Mustang Island State Park, just a 15-minute drive south of Port Aransas.

Animal lovers will be drawn to the lost wild horses, called *mesteños,* in nearby Mustang Island State Park. Legend has it that in the 1820s, famed pirate Jean Lafitte drove a spiked Spanish dagger into the sand somewhere on Mustang Island, marking the spot of a buried treasure of gold and jewels. Today, a kayaking trip along the 20-mile-long Mustang Island Paddling Trail will showcase the beauty of the park and provides a great chance to spot the island's robust population of seabirds. The beaches offer pristine expanses for sunbathing and splashing in the water (though you should really keep an eye out for that buried treasure). There are also 48 electric hookup and potable water campsites and 50 primitive sites available on or near the beach if you'd like to spend a night under the stars here.

The beautiful redbrick Aransas Pass Lighthouse, also known as Lydia Ann, stands on the Texas Gulf Coast near Port A. On the National Register of Historic Places, it changed hands between Confederate and Union forces in the Civil War and has withstood years of hurricane damage since its construction in the mid-1800s. The lighthouse is only accessible by surrounding waterways and not available for tours, but the chattering dolphins and colorful fish that swim alongside the boats make the trip to see this piece of Texas history a worthwhile journey nonetheless.

ROUND TOP

TEXAS

Not everything is bigger in Texas. But what the tiny town of Round Top lacks in size, it makes up for in personality. Best known for the Original Round Top Antiques Fair (aka "the Show"), as well as the fancier Marburger Farm Antique Show in the spring and fall, Round Top is a place where designers, home decor enthusiasts, and scavengers flock. During the Show, hundreds of vendors from all over the world line more than 11 miles of fields along Highway 237. The triannual event is attended by more than 100,000 people.

Forward-thinking hoteliers and restaurateurs have created top-notch lodging and dining options in Round Top. The Frenchie is an eclectic boutique hotel set in a renovated 1800s farmhouse, blending small-town Texas charm with a chic French-forward design. The quirky, whimsical compound called Rancho Pillow provides playful accommodations, most notably an 18th-century Dutch barn turned weekend escape that was transported from its original home in upstate New York. Oversize neon guitar installations mix with hand-hewn hemlock frame timbers to create a magical place to stay.

In Round Top proper, grab a glass of wine at Prost on Block 29, a wine bar housed in a historic stone cottage. Or for a special evening out, cozy up on a vintage green velvet banquette at Lulu's and indulge in an excellent Italian meal. Vintage Americana with a bohemian splash best describes a weekend getaway to Round Top—one you surely won't forget.

The Marburger Farm Antique Show in Round Top hosts 300 vendors across an area large enough to accommodate five football fields.

TASTE OF THE REGION

TEXAS TRASH PIE

Royers Round Top Cafe in Texas Hill Country is considered the home of Texas trash pie, which is made with a sweet and salty combination of baking staples and classic snack foods. The pie filling includes chocolate chips, crushed pretzels and graham crackers, shredded coconut, pecans, and caramel, all mixed together with melted butter and sweetened condensed milk. Many Texans make this pie at home, but it is worth a trip to Royers in Round Top to taste the original.

WIMBERLEY

TEXAS

Escape the Texas heat by jumping into a crystal clear swimming hole near Wimberley. Most famous among these hidden gems is the distinctive Blue Hole, a natural swimming area shaded by majestic cypress trees and fed by the temperate waters of Cypress Creek in Blue Hole Regional Park. A picnic and a dip in the water during the designated swimming season (May to September) are essential to experiencing a classic Wimberley afternoon. Nearby is Jacob's Well Natural Area, a swimming hole created from the artisan spring and underground cave system of Trinity Aquifer. The caves transport cool water from 140 feet below the earth's surface, but instead of what would probably be a frightening dive, you can hike the walkways crisscrossing the park and jump off surrounding rocks into the water.

Wimberley embodies the beauty of Texas Hill Country. Cypress Creek and the Blanco River converge near the center of town, which started as a trading post settlement in 1848. Towering cypress trees shape the landscape, and visitors delight in the Texas bluebonnets in full bloom on the rolling hills from late March through April. For a bird's-eye view of the Frio River Canyon and Wimberley Valley, hike the 218-step limestone staircase to the top of Prayer Mountain, better known as "Old Baldy."

The charm of the town itself gives the beautiful scenery a run for its money. Locally painted six-to-eight-foot-tall cowboy boot sculptures are

Visit the spring at Jacob's Well Natural Area for outdoor fun in the warmer months. When the water level is high enough, visitors can swim.

ADVENTURE ALONG THE WAY

DEVIL'S BACKBONE SCENIC DRIVE

It's rumored that the ghosts of Spanish monks, Confederate soldiers, and Native Americans haunt this scenic loop along a limestone ridge running through Texas Hill Country. Haunted or not, this remarkable drive has epic views of the Balcones Fault, along with curvy roads dotted by cacti and junipers. The best time of year for a drive is early spring, when Texas bluebonnets are in bloom.

A striking boot by artist Tiffany O'Neill Huff greets visitors to Wimberley's Wild West Store, where you can browse more than 500 pairs of vintage boots (by appointment only).

displayed throughout downtown. These "Bootiful" boots celebrate the arts and culture in Wimberley, with wildflowers, cowboys, and cactus sunset scenes hand painted on each. Wimberley Square, the heart of downtown, looks as if it were plucked off a movie set. Limestone facades and colorful clapboard buildings house boutiques featuring locally crafted goods, and visitors will hear country, blues, and folk music wafting from various live music venues most days. Cypress Creek flows through the square, creating an atmosphere that is both serene and energetic. Walk the Gallery Trail Wimberley to visit with local artists and craftspeople.

A few minutes out of town is the Shady Llama, a 35-acre ranch housing a pack of roaming llamas plus a fabulous outdoor wine-and-beer garden. Grab a bite from the Deli Llama food truck and enjoy a crisp pint of craft beer while taking in the beautiful hillside view. On the opposite end of town is Roughhouse Brewing, an award-winning craft brewery set on a family-owned 50-acre ranch. An old red pickup truck with artfully placed cacti sits in front of a weathered wood barn. Live music on the Lantana Stage in the desert garden creates a perfectly Texan taproom environment. Nearby is Wimberley Glassworks, a glass-blowing studio established in 1992. Live demonstrations and art installations make it impossible *not* to pick up a gorgeous handblown platter or pitcher to take a piece of Wimberley home.

West Stor
SELL · TRADE
Home of the
BOOT WHISPERER

PART FOUR

MIDWEST

Marietta, Ohio (seen here; page 272), and Williamstown, West Virginia, face each other across the Ohio River.

GALENA

ILLINOIS

Outdoor enthusiasts and avid birders will find a special treat in Galena: the Galena River Trail, which boasts a vast array of wildlife. But the river trail is just a primer for all that this town has to offer during a weekend getaway.

The Galena River Trail is perfect for biking and traversing wooded areas, farmlands, and bluffs. Veer slightly off the trail up Bouthillier Street to visit the Ulysses S. Grant Home, a 19th-century Italianate house with the original furnishings from the 18th president of the United States. Grant had an outsize presence in Galena, his hometown. After the Civil War, the decorated general returned here to organize his presidential campaign. Grant chose downtown's DeSoto House, an 1855 hotel, as his campaign headquarters (rooms 209 and 211 to be exact). Today, visitors can stay amid history within its original brick walls and beamed ceilings. Eat at the Green Street Tavern, at its current location since 1883, which boasts great views of Main Street.

Affectionately dubbed the Helluva Half Mile, Galena's historic Main Street looks nearly the same as it did in its Civil War–era heyday, when major politicians such as Abraham Lincoln campaigned in the area. You can window-shop at Main Street's more than 100 storefronts, with their 19th-century brick facades, and stop in art galleries, museums, and restaurants. More than 85 percent of town is on the National Register of Historic Places, and Galena

Birders might spot male indigo buntings like this one in the azalea bushes around Galena.

TASTE OF THE REGION

POPCORN

Popcorn is the official state snack of Illinois, a nod to the hundreds of state farms that grow corn. The road to this designation began in 2003, when second- and third-grade classes from Cunningham Elementary School in Joliet lobbied the general assembly to make the designation. Of course, there's no one designated way to cook or season popcorn; luckily, it tastes delicious whether served sweet or savory.

Main Street in historic downtown Galena features more than 125 shops and restaurants.

has done an excellent job of retaining its charm while retrofitting old factories and businesses into modern-day offerings including shops like the Scent Workshop and Galena Book and Paper.

The historic Ulysses Suites, housed in the J. G. Schmohl building, still offers "rooms for tourists," just as it did in the 1920s and '30s when it was known as the Grant Hotel. Fully renovated with an eye toward luxury, rooms at the Ulysses put lodgers just steps from Main Street in accommodations with tasteful exposed brick, claw-foot tubs, and curated furnishings. Meanwhile, the Inn at Irish Hollow is one of Galena's more romantic lodging options, tucked away in the countryside. Hand-hewn beams and wood-burning limestone fireplaces make the private English cottages on the 500-acre property feel straight out of a storybook.

For an excursion outside town, take the Stagecoach Trail to reach Galena Cellars Vineyard and Winery, where a charmingly weathered red barn with a sloped roof and cathedral-style windows sits among rows of grapevines. Three generations of the Lawlor-White family have run this successful winery; varietals like Eric the Red, made from estate-grown Marechal Foch grapes, fly out the door as soon as they're in stock. In town, the vineyard's newly opened tasting room in the center of Main Street is a community gathering spot and a great place to enjoy a wine flight or cocktail while enjoying live music.

PUBLIC RESTROOMS
VISITOR CENTER
cafe
INN
3 HR PARKING DAILY 9AM TO 5PM
NO PARKING 2AM TO 6AM TUE & THU
HANDICAPPED PARKING
PERMIT REQUIRED
Coffee Shop

GALENA
VINEYARD &

OPPOSITE TOP: Horseshoe Mound Preserve offers scenic views across Illinois, Iowa, and Wisconsin. **OPPOSITE BOTTOM:** The Presidential Suite at Ulysses Suites pays tribute to the 18th U.S. president. **LEFT:** Lodging, live music on weekends, and tastings await at Galena Cellars Vineyard and Winery.

For a truly quirky outdoor excursion, hike alongside a friendly herd of goats with Hoof It Goat Treks. Wooded acres and rolling prairies make up the family-owned property, and there is something uniquely immersive about hand-feeding goats while exploring the grounds. For more traditional hiking, Horseshoe Mound Preserve is just up the road, offering panoramic views of Illinois, Iowa, and Wisconsin—a true midwestern vista. A manicured gathering circle at Horseshoe Mound greets explorers with a classic parklike feel; as one ventures farther into the park, the landscape becomes wilder. Meteors can be seen shooting across the sky on a clear evening—they're usually best viewed after midnight. Limited light pollution in the area allows for ideal viewing conditions.

ADVENTURE ALONG THE WAY

THE GREAT RIVER ROAD

The Great River Road follows the Mississippi River through 10 states. Across 3,000 miles, drivers will take in beautiful bluffs and riverbanks. The 550-mile Illinois leg goes right through Galena, passing local wineries and breweries, as well as pick-your-own farms, state parks, and historic sites. It's a true all-American adventure.

DOUGLAS

OTTAWA

ILLINOIS

Ottawa is in the heart of LaSalle County in northern Illinois. The charming town is close to several major cities and is considered the hub for four state parks, including the locally beloved Starved Rock State Park. Come for the outdoor adventure, and stay for Ottawa's welcoming atmosphere.

Downtown Ottawa presents a visual history of the area via incredibly detailed murals, some of which span entire sides of buildings. "Day of the Great Debate" by artist Don Gray, for example, commemorates the first debate between presidential candidates Abraham Lincoln and Stephen A. Douglas, which took place in Ottawa's Washington Square Park in August 1858. At the time, hundreds of people showed up to see Lincoln's breakthrough appearance, and today the beautifully maintained park is filled with colorful gardens and spirited fountains, along with bronze statues of Lincoln and Douglas.

This mural of Abraham Lincoln and Stephen A. Douglas, just off Washington Square Park, commemorates the site of the first famed Lincoln-Douglas debate.

The impressive 50-foot-tall Reddick Mansion anchors the park; built in 1855, it is an incredibly preserved piece of pre–Civil War architecture, and it was among the most expensive and ornately built private homes in Illinois at the time. You can take a guided tour of the home's 22 rooms or attend a seasonal event.

Outside Ottawa, former cornfields and beanfields have been restored to tallgrass prairie at Dayton Bluffs Preserve, an effort to restore the landscape to the way wild Illinois appeared hundreds of years ago. Seeing wild turkeys and white-tailed deer among butterflies and birds provides a hopeful example of the potential for nature preservation. The sacred Native American burial mounds within the preserve are a reminder of the site's history, necessity, and significance.

Tangled Roots Brewing Company draws from Ottawa's natural surroundings, serving "farm to foam" craft beer alongside seasonal fare at the Lone Buffalo. The taste of Ottawa is as simple as a freshly brewed hoppy IPA paired with a hearty sandwich or steak with locally sourced and expertly prepared veggies on the side.

MADISON

INDIANA

Springtime in Madison, Indiana, is an explosion of color. Pink and white cherry blossoms line dazzling Riverfront Park along the banks of the Ohio River, accenting the exceptionally preserved architecture in the downtown area, which has been tagged a national historic landmark district. The ornate, patinaed 19th-century Broadway Fountain, just off Main Street, is a true treasure of Indiana that was saved by the community and rededicated in 1980 for the nation's bicentennial celebration. The crown jewel of the historic district is the Lanier Mansion. The ochre-colored Greek Revival masterpiece, built in 1844, is set along the river amid a flowering garden. Inside the mansion, check out the iconic self-supporting spiral staircase and the intricate, hand-stamped botanical wallpaper.

Impressive federal-style brick buildings line the main thoroughfare. Among the highlights are the "Kindness" mural, a colorful backdrop for Instagrammers, and boutiques like Olde Tyme Marketplace. Take a walk down Main Street on a Saturday morning to visit the oldest farmers market in Indiana, dating back to 1809.

Just a few miles west of downtown sits Clifty Falls State Park. Its namesake cascade is never more majestic than after a rainfall, when water levels are at their peak. The park overlooks the Ohio River and is filled with million-year-old shale and limestone rocks. Springtime is ideal for a visit, as rains and the subsequent growing season create a lush landscape for hiking and camping.

Clifty Falls State Park is best visited in the winter or spring, when the falls are at their most powerful.

TALK LIKE A LOCAL

"HOOSIER"

Back in the early 1800s, referring to someone as a "Hoosier" implied that they were unrefined, with a frontier roughness deemed uncivilized. However, since the mid-1840s, the descriptor has shifted into a term of endearment and pride. Indiana University adopted the Hoosier name for its athletic teams, and the term is now a moniker of friendliness, neighborliness, and an idyllic contentment with Indiana life.

VESTERHEIM
Embellishment
Supported by
The Iowa Arts Council, a division of the Iowa Department of Cultural Affairs
The National Endowment for the Arts
VESTERHEIM
A Fine Art Exhibit
VESTERHEIM
NORWEGIAN
AMERICAN
MUSEUM
VESTERHEIM
Sámi Dreams:
Portraits of Resilience in the Norwegian Arctic

DECORAH

IOWA

Limestone bluffs, tree-covered valleys, and the Upper Iowa River surround the town of Decorah, where outdoor adventure mixes seamlessly with great eats and rich heritage.

Visit Vesterheim, the National Norwegian-American Museum and Folk Art School, to see the world's largest collection of Norwegian American artifacts and experience the stories of Decorah's earliest settlers. Classes are available at the Folk Art School, with options like rosemaling (Scandinavian-style painted or carved decorations), fiber arts, and woodworking. Or come to Decorah in July, when Nordic Fest further celebrates the town's Scandinavian heritage.

For a full tour of town, bike the Trout Run Trail. This route winds through the 19th- and early 20th-century buildings in Decorah's downtown district before tracing the Upper Iowa River and looping through a series of country-road switchbacks. It's a not-too-difficult 11-mile ride (or hike or run) that shows off the rugged beauty of northeast Iowa.

Grab a bite at Luna Valley Farm, known locally as "Decorah's backyard." The farm hosts pizza nights, when owners Maren and Tom Beard bring the community together for wood-fired artisan pies topped with ingredients grown on the farm or by neighbors. On the farm, a rustic red barn sits among rolling green hills, and families and friends spread out on the lawn or at picnic tables to unwind and eat.

Vesterheim, the National Norwegian-American Museum and Folk Art School, exhibits settler artifacts, art, and woodwork.

ADVENTURE ALONG THE WAY

SEED SAVERS EXCHANGE HERITAGE FARM

Colorful blooms burst from the 890 scenic acres of the Seed Savers Exchange Heritage Farm just outside Decorah. Ruby moon hyacinth beans, garden huckleberries, Mexican sunflowers, and Bulls Blood beets are just a small sample of the 1,000 plants grown each year on the farm. The property also houses a seed bank of more than 20,000 plant varieties. Hiking trails wind through the rolling hills alongside rivers and streams, and the Lillian Goldman Visitors Center sells seeds to grow back at home.

PELLA

IOWA

In the 1840s, a group of around 800 Dutch immigrants came to central Iowa to escape religious persecution. They called their settlement Pella, after the name of a biblical city of refuge. Many descendants of the original founders still reside here today, occasionally speaking in Pella Dutch, a subdialect of South Guelderish. Strong ties to Dutch culture can be found all over town. The Vermeer windmill, standing proudly as a centerpiece downtown, was designed and built in the Netherlands, then disassembled, shipped to Pella, and reassembled here in 2002. Tours of this working grain mill are available most days, and the view from the top of the observation deck shows off the Historical Village, a collection of period-specific buildings depicting life in Pella in the 1850s. A clog-cobbler shop, a smithy, and a sod house populate the grounds, making it feel as though you've stepped back in time and into another part of the world.

The Tulip Time Festival celebrates the area's Dutch heritage every May, when more than 300,000 tulips bloom at once.

The community of Pella innately gives off *gezellig*—a Dutch term for the companionable, homey, and convivial vibe at the heart of the culture. Cozy up at either Vander Ploeg Bakery or Jaarsma Bakery for a traditional treat, like a *banketletter* (an S-shaped puff pastry filled with almond paste, also known as a Dutch letter) or a *poffertjes* mini pancake. Find more European charm in Molengracht Plaza, which is modeled after an authentic Dutch square and sits catty-corner to Central Park.

TASTE OF THE REGION

RING BOLOGNA

You'll spot ring bologna all over Pella—it's kind of a thing here. This Dutch-inspired smoked meat comes in a signature horseshoe shape, but Pella's version is smaller and snack friendly, appropriate for slicing to go on a cheese board, top a cracker, or tuck into a cozy casserole. Ulrich Meat Market has been making theirs for more than 150 years, and just down the street, In't Veld's Meat Market has sold their version from the same location since 1941.

Molengracht Plaza was designed to replicate an authentic Dutch square, including a 5,270-square-foot canal.

Walk along its winding blue canal and brick-laden promenade, stopping to shop at charming boutiques like Blush and Simple Hōm for modern boho-chic Scandinavian pieces, or to enjoy confections and clog-shaped treats at Van Veen Chocolates. Artisanal markets such as Ulrich Meat Market and Frisian Farms Cheese House offer delectable bologna and Gouda, respectively.

Each May in Pella, a kaleidoscope of hundreds of thousands of colorful tulips bloom, signifying the beginning of the annual Tulip Time Festival, which takes place over the first weekend of the month. Drawing crowds from all over Iowa—and the country—Tulip Time celebrates Pella's Dutch heritage with 300,000 blooms as the backdrop, culminating in the highly anticipated Volks Parade. Dutch-inspired floats ride down the streets with lively bands and costumed marchers in wooden *klompen* (clogs). The Tulip Queen and her court, selected from among a group of nominated local high school seniors, are crowned. Tulips fill flower boxes, garden beds, and Tulip Avenue in Central Park, which has 83 different varieties of the flower. Tulip bulbs shipped directly from the Netherlands are available for purchase. It's quite the event, and an excellent time to visit this slice of the old country in America's heartland.

Pella WINDOWS &

LINDSBORG

KANSAS

Downtown Lindsborg is best known for its collection of fiberglass horses, the famed Wild Dala Herd, which signify this Kansas town's pride and artistic bent. Dala horses are carved and painted wooden horses traditionally made in Sweden's Dalarna region. In Lindsborg, the horses are sponsored by local businesses or community members and painted in unconventional patterns. They serve as both unique community logos and symbols of *välkommen* (welcome).

Nearly half of Lindsborg's residents have Swedish ancestors, and celebrations like Vaffeldagen (Waffle Day) in March, Midsummer's Festival at the summer solstice, Svensk Hyllningsfest in October, and St. Lucia at the winter solstice celebrate this collective heritage. The arts flourish in Lindsborg: The Red Barn Studio Museum features sculptures and paintings by Lester Raymer, Hemslöjd (Swedish for "handicraft") is a workshop for Dala horses, and the Birger Sandzén Memorial Gallery exhibits works from the world-famous artist known for depicting Kansas and Southwest landscapes.

For Swedish delicacies, try lingonberry applesauce and artisan-forged coffee at the Blacksmith coffeehouse, located in a renovated blacksmith shop. White's Foodliner stocks authentic Swedish foods, including Swedish potato sausage and chewy fish-shaped candies. For apparel, Ivory Thimble sells traditional Swedish clothing and sewing patterns.

Lindsborg's Wild Dala Herd celebrates the town's Swedish American heritage. Each of these horses is decorated by a local artist and receives an unveiling party by the community.

ADVENTURE ALONG THE WAY

CORONADO HEIGHTS PARK

Spanish coins from bygone wilderness explorers have been found at the southern bluff of Coronado Heights in the Smoky Hills of Kansas, just 10 minutes northwest of Lindsborg. The sandstone castle rising high above the landscape is named after Spanish explorer Francisco Vásquez de Coronado, who visited the region in 1541 in search of the mythical seven cities of gold. His less-than-fruitful expedition may have ended in Coronado Heights, which today is a beautiful picnic spot, especially to watch the sun set over the prairie.

HORN'S
BAR
Millie's on Main
Great Turtle Toys
Shirt Off My Back
3-D
DICKS FUDGE

MACKINAC ISLAND

MICHIGAN

Formerly called Fort Mackinac, for the British stronghold built in 1780, Mackinac Island (pronounced MACK-in-awe) is an idyllic enclave on Lake Huron between Michigan's Upper and Lower Peninsulas. An 18-minute ferry ride brings visitors to the shores of a car-free town spanning just four square miles within Mackinac Island State Park. In 1875, the island became the nation's second ever national park (after Yellowstone) before its administration was eventually transferred to the state of Michigan in 1895. Beautifully preserved green space and historic buildings offer a midwestern summer destination worth returning to year after year.

Worldly worries simply melt away the moment the ferry docks in the harbor, and the hospitality is palpable throughout the island community. To get a lay of the land, some of the best views in town can be had from the perch of the classic white rocking chairs along the iconic 660-foot-long porch of the Grand Hotel, which sits on a bluff overlooking the turquoise blue waters of the Straits of Mackinac. Facing west, the porch is an excellent spot to catch a sunset. A national historic landmark, the hotel and its fragrant lilac bushes and rolling green lawns have welcomed out-of-towners since 1887, now marrying old-world sophistication with luxurious modern charm. Dog-friendly Mission Point Resort sits on the "sunrise side" of the island. Adirondack chairs and colorful tulips, shaded

Bikes are the most common transportation you'll see on Mackinac Island, where cars are not allowed.

TASTE OF THE REGION

CONEY DOG

Topped with beef chili, yellow mustard, and diced white onions, Michigan's version of a Coney Island hot dog is different from New York's but has roots in the Empire State. The theory is that Greek immigrants passed through Coney Island on their way to Detroit, then proceeded to open diners serving a midwestern take on the beloved hot dog, named in homage to the fare they enjoyed back East. Today, the loaded dogs are just as much a Michigan staple as they are an icon of New York City.

Arch Rock on Mackinac Island stretches more than 50 feet across. Visitors can reach the formation for photo ops on foot, by bike, or in a horse-drawn taxi.

under cedar and paper birch trees, overlook the water's edge.

Nearly 80 percent of the island is part of Mackinac Island State Park, with preserved hardwood forests, limestone rock formations, and sea caves. By land or by sea, Arch Rock is one of the most recognizable features. The natural eyehole limestone formation frames Lake Huron perfectly. A hike takes explorers right up to the rock (no climbing allowed), while a kayak trip provides a lower-level viewpoint. Seventy miles of unpaved and natural trails crisscross the landscape. Crack-in-the-Island is just what its name indicates—a literal crack in the limestone foundation of the island that hikers can shimmy through. Also check out the nearby Cave of the Woods, hollowed out hundreds of years ago by waves crashing into the rock. The Point Lookout Trail is a lesser known hike that delivers a bird's-eye view of the island and the unique Sugar Loaf limestone stack, surrounded by lush spruce and white pine trees. The restored Fort Mackinac serves as headquarters for the park. It's worth exploring the Revolutionary War–era barracks and Avenue of Flags for a look at how this strategic stronghold influenced U.S. history. If you want more relaxed recreation, horses and bicycles are the main modes of transportation on the island—even the mail is delivered by horse-drawn dray.

It seems that no visitor can leave Mackinac Island without sampling the famous fudge found at one of the dozens of candy shops downtown, earning

No-Nut
tter
Nut
alnut
Mackin

OPPOSITE TOP: The annual Lilac Festival is the ideal time for a horse-drawn carriage ride. **OPPOSITE BOTTOM:** Sunset on Lake Michigan invites views of the marina and Saint Anne's Catholic Church. **LEFT:** Ryba's Fudge Shops have been family operated on the island since 1960.

out-of-towners the nickname "fudgies." Mackinac Island is affectionately called "America's fudge capital," and the Fudge Festival in August brings the entire island together in sweet delight. Fudge tastings, beer-and-fudge pairings, horse-drawn floats, and fudgemaking demonstrations honor the treat, which has been a staple of the island since the Victorian era. In June, the beloved Lilac Festival showcases the island in bloom, with pale purple to vibrant magenta flowers packing the landscape. Live music fills the streets during the Grand Parade, eager gardeners can attend lilac-planting seminars, and the Lilac Queen coronation honors local students who have given back to the community.

TALK LIKE A LOCAL

"THE MITTEN"

Ask a Michigander where they are from, and they'll inevitably hold up their hand to point to a spot on "the Mitten," a rudimentary map named for the approximate shape of the state's landmass. The eastern region of Michigan is "the Thumb," and the state capital, Lansing, is near the middle. One shortfall of the mitten map is that it doesn't include Michigan's Upper Peninsula, whose residents will tell you they are from "the U.P."

ST. JOSEPH

MICHIGAN

The West Michigan Pike is often called "the Riviera of the Midwest." The historic byway connects the state's most picturesque beach towns along Lake Michigan. One of the best of these beachside havens is St. Joseph, or St. Joe for those in the know. Summer days on St. Joe are filled with families enjoying the hot sun and lazy lake breeze at Silver Beach County Park, which is walking distance from downtown. Near the beach is the Whirlpool Compass Fountain, an interactive splash pad that delights kids looking to cool off. The sounds of the vintage organ at the Silver Beach Carousel fill the air.

You'll want to make your way to Tiscornia Park to see its dual North Pier lighthouses. The Inner and Outer Lights, both constructed in the early 1900s, are connected by a pier that extends a few hundred feet into the lake waters. Built to usher vessels into the St. Joseph River from Lake Michigan, the lighthouses are an iconic feature of the town. In the summer, the sloping moraines meet a backdrop of blue water, while in the winter, massive icicles crystallize along the pier. Another welcoming beacon along the water is "And You, Seas," a stunning abstract stainless-steel sculpture by Richard Hunt that stretches almost 50 feet tall.

The sandy loam soil, moderate spring temperatures, and the proximity to Lake Michigan have

The Silver Beach Carousel continues a century-old tradition of amusement in St. Joseph.

ADVENTURE ALONG THE WAY

HISTORIC FISHTOWN

Michigan's fishing heritage is preserved at Historic Fishtown in Leland, a shoreside town on the northwestern coast of Lake Michigan, four hours from St. Joe. Weathered fishing shanties, docks, and smokehouses are evidence of the maritime culture that helped build the state. Fish tugs commissioned in 1958 named *Janice Sue* and *Mary Ann*—the first steel-hulled, rather than wooden, boats in Leland—sit in the harbor, and adorable otters swim in the river. Grab a bite of fresh seafood to eat on a dock, shop at the galleries and boutiques tucked into charming weather-beaten buildings, and head out on the water for chance to reel in the catch of the day.

The Whirlpool Compass Fountain runs on a set schedule throughout the spring, summer, and fall.

created an ideal fruit-growing region around St. Joe. The Blossomtime Festival, hosted by St. Joseph and neighboring Benton Harbor, has celebrated the springtime arrival of orchard blossoms since 1906. Peaches, sweet Niagara grapes, and tart cherries fill market stands; Mr. and Miss Blossomtime wave atop parade floats; and the Run for the Buds 5K brings crowds in the thousands each year.

Surrounding wineries also benefit from the temperate growing conditions, producing grapes similar to those found in the Loire Valley in France. The Lake Michigan Shore Wine Trail weaves past 15 quality wineries that add distinct Michigan character to classics like chardonnay and cabernet sauvignon. The red barn and tree-shaded lawn at Hickory Creek Winery welcomes oenophiles for tastings seven days a week. Wispy deer grass frames a picnic area with firepit seating, while a vintage tractor and tire swing create a pastoral country scene. Try Hickory Creek's apple wine for something sweet or a Merlot-Carménère for something zesty.

The downtown district in St. Joe is the place to kick back. At 221 Main, grab a cocktail on the terrace for views of bustling Main Street, then head to Silver Beach Pizza, housed in an old train depot, for some of the best slices in southwest Michigan. A short walk along St. Joe's brick streets leads to Box Factory for the Arts, a rehabbed factory with multiple galleries. It hosts free exhibits, live performances, and an art market selling local and regional works.

GRAND MARAIS

MINNESOTA

Traditionally rigged steel schooners called *hjørdis* sail across chilly Lake Superior near Grand Marais. These flagship vessels, available for rent through the North House Folk School, embody the mix of outdoor adventure and creativity that this harbor town is known for. Quirky Grand Marais (pronounced MAH-ray) sits on land originally inhabited by the Ojibwe people, who used the area as a summer village. Today, outdoor enthusiasts use it as a gateway to the Boundary Waters Canoe Area Wilderness, a vast network of 1,100 lakes and 1,500 miles of paddling routes along the U.S.-Canada border. These waters are an ideal place to witness the northern lights. For a daytime adventure, float alongside pristine quaking aspen, red pine, and balsam poplar forests.

The beauty of the rugged landscape weaves through Grand Marais. The old Light Keeper's House is the best place to watch the sunset from the shore of Lake Superior. For a bird's-eye view of Grand Marais Harbor, hike up the narrow wilderness path of the Sweetheart's Bluff Trail on the far western edge of the Grand Marais Recreation Area. Along the way is a clearing with exposed basalt rock showing scars from glaciers that receded millennia ago.

Artists and nonconformists have been drawn to Grand Marais for decades. The Grand Marais Art Colony has fostered experimentation and self-discovery among contemporary artists since 1947. Today, the Arts Festival in July brings the community together with live music, great food, and an outdoor market featuring artists' wares. Inspired by Scandinavian *folkehøjskolers* (folk schools), the North House Folk School offers workshops on timber framing, coiled-basket-making, Inuit kayak building, and other traditional northern crafts to help preserve the town's heritage.

A visit to Grand Marais is not complete without a stop at World's Best Donuts. The landmark red-and-white shop is family owned and known for its mouthwatering cake doughnuts, skizzles (sweet, fried yeast dough), and doughnut kabobs.

Take a sunset cruise on Lake Superior aboard a schooner from Grand Marais Harbor.

USAF

STILLWATER

MINNESOTA

Stillwater, right along Minnesota's border with Wisconsin, is at the southern end of the St. Croix River, a national scenic riverway whose smooth waters reflect lush green wooded bluffs. Logging put Stillwater on the map—at one point, the town's lumber mills were the largest producer in the country. Wealth from the logging boom subsequently brought railroads, steamships, and grand homes. The town became so influential that in 1848 it was selected to hold a convention on the corner of Myrtle and Main Streets to petition for Minnesota to be recognized as a U.S. territory. Eventually, Stillwater shifted from logging town to tourist getaway, but the preservation of the historic community remains at the forefront. The annual Lumberjack Days festival celebrates the town's cultural heritage with a parade, a downhill derby, and lumberjack demonstrations.

Visit the iconic Stillwater Lift Bridge, built in 1931, which spans the St. Croix and connects Stillwater to Houlton, Wisconsin. It's worth taking a stroll over the bridge for phenomenal views of the river. To experience the calm waters firsthand, head out on a sunset cruise on an old-fashioned riverboat. For a more hands-on way to explore, launch your own kayak into the Lower St. Croix River or link up with a local outfitter for a guided paddle.

The Stillwater Commercial Historic District is listed on the National Register of Historic Places. Browse boutiques like Smith and Trade Mercantile

The Lumberjack Days festival includes music, food, games, and impressive demonstrations of lumberjack skills.

TASTE OF THE REGION

HOT DISH

While outsiders might argue that a hot dish and a casserole are essentially the same thing, Minnesotans *cannot* be convinced. The classic hot dish began in the 1930s as a farmwives' solution for an easy-to-prepare and economical meal. A popular version today has a filling of ground beef, cream-of-mushroom soup, corn, peas, and cheese, all topped with Tater Tots and baked to a golden brown. A serving of this hot dish is perfect for warming up on a chilly winter night. This is true comfort food.

The Washington County Historic Courthouse is now a museum, gallery, and event space; its grounds make a great photo op.

for local artisanal goods, and stop by Candyland for its famous Chicago-mix popcorn (cheddar and caramel). To travel between the historic sites in town and the bluffs, there are five outdoor staircases; the Main Street stairs take climbers to a vista overlooking the river. Continue your walking tour by heading to the oldest standing courthouse in the state: the Washington County Historic Courthouse. Now a museum, gallery, and event space, the impressive redbrick Greek Revival building is visible throughout most of downtown and can orient any first-time visitors who get turned around.

Stay at the urban yet rustic Hotel Crosby, where beds sit on frames made from wooden beams, exposed brick is highlighted with ironwork, and buttery soft leather armchairs flank a roaring fireplace. It's a luxury retreat just steps from Main Street. The dog-friendly Lora Hotel was built on the foundation of the 1868 Joseph Wolf Brewery on the banks of the St. Croix. Stone walls and secret cave entrances create a romantic vibe. You'll find unexpected flavors at Feller, the in-house restaurant, and craft cocktails at its bar, The Long Goodbye. River Siren Brewing, one of the many microbreweries in town, pays homage to the Stillwater legend of a mysterious maiden who lured loggers away from the shoreline with her siren song. Beers such as the Sailor's Destruction IPA and Foggy Abyss oatmeal stout recall her tale and pay homage to the surrounding waters that gave the town its name.

OPPOSITE TOP: This Myrtle Street mural honors the town's roots in the lumber industry. OPPOSITE BOTTOM: Lora Hotel features the cozy bar Long Goodbye. LEFT: Pedestrians and cyclists can traverse the St. Croix Crossing Bridge as part of a 4.7-mile loop trail.

For outdoor adventurers, Stillwater serves as the hub for more than 100 miles of biking trails. Riders can hop on the Brown's Creek Trail in Stillwater for a six-mile ride to the Gateway State Trail, an 18-mile paved pathway that runs from Pine Point Regional Park to St. Paul along what was once the Soo Line Railroad. A canopy of silver maple and green ash trees shade the path, with pale purple hepatica flowers peeking from the forest bed. The St. Croix River Crossing Loop Trail connects Minnesota and Wisconsin over the Stillwater Lift Bridge and the new St. Croix Crossing Bridge in a 4.7-mile loop.

Come winter, many of the trails turn into routes for cross-country skiing and snowshoeing. For a classic cold-weather outing, lace up your skates at the family-friendly seasonal outdoor ice rink in front of the Water Street Inn, where you can glide along and enjoy views of the St. Croix River.

TALK LIKE A LOCAL

"DUCK, DUCK, GRAY DUCK"

While most kindergartners play "duck, duck, goose," in Minnesota it's "duck, duck, gray duck." Taggers announce colors of ducks (blue duck, yellow duck) until deeming someone the gray duck. Trickery and deceit play an outsize role in this version of the playground game: Savvy players throw out "gold duck" and "green duck" to expose twitchy participants.

HERMANNHOF
CHARDONEL

HERMANN

MISSOURI

A rich midwestern tradition of viticulture is fostered in the town of Hermann. Seven total wineries call this Missouri enclave home, and for a brief time in the late 1860s, Hermann was the country's biggest wine producer. When a group of German immigrants settled Hermann in 1837, they found an area similar to the Rhine River Valley. Naturally, grapes were the crop that grew best here, too. Modern visitors can experience this heritage at the Hermann Farm Museum, which spans a collection of historic buildings, including the Teubner-Husmann House, home of George Husmann, the father of Missouri wine. Shire horses graze in lush paddocks throughout the farm, which also serves as a preservation site for these majestic and gentle animals, a breed designated critical by the Livestock Conservancy due to their limited population numbers.

For a bit of wine history, take a self-guided tasting trip along the Hermann Wine Trail through the rolling Missouri countryside. Adam Puchta Winery, established in 1855, has been passed down through seven generations. Its expansive lawn is filled with red-roofed barns surrounded by canopies of dogwood, hickory, and maple trees, a prime setting for live music and an afternoon of sipping dry Vignoles. Hermannhof Winery, housed in a stately brick building on the edge of downtown, has a beautiful outdoor patio with views of the Missouri River. Its award-winning wines celebrate the Germanic influence of the town's earliest founders.

For exercise, bike along Katy Trail State Park, a former railroad track turned 240-mile path that offers beautiful views of Missouri farm fields. For lodging, stay connected with nature in a luxury tree house at the Cottage, where you can soak in the greenery on the elevated porches and walkways and enjoy a different breakfast menu every morning, or pick a historic stone cottage on a hillside at the Inn at Hermannhof. Dating back to the first settlers in the 1830s, these fully restored winehouses blend historic charm with modern luxury and are just a short walk from the heart of downtown.

At the Inn at Hermannhof, certain room packages offer bottles and snacks from the Hermannhof Winery.

ITCHEN

WESTON

MISSOURI

Apple butter, apple dumplings, and apple pies abound during Applefest, one of the best fall festivals in Missouri and the premier event in historic Weston. Come for the delicious apple-themed festivities and live apple butter-making demonstration, and bustling activities, then stay to experience the rest of what Weston has to offer.

Visitors can get their fall fix at Weston Red Barn Farm, a bucolic working farm with rolling acres of pumpkin patches and apple orchards, an original tobacco barn turned country store, and a corn maze. For another made-in-Weston experience, check out the award-winning sheep milk cheeses at Green Dirt Farm Creamery, where you can enjoy fresh air and farm-to-table goods, including artisanal cheeses and ice cream, while strolling the property.

Weston, situated on a bluff overlooking the Missouri River, was established as a market center for the surrounding agricultural region, where tobacco and hemp were once the main crops. The town continues to celebrate parts of its past. The Holladay Distillery runs a tasting room on Main Street as well as a full production facility near Weston Bend State Park. Founded in 1856, it is the oldest distillery west of the Mississippi River still operating in its original location. Experience an authentic taste of Missouri on a tour of the distillery or by grabbing a fresh cocktail at the location downtown. Just off

Bagpipers lead the Applefest Parade. Stay the entire Applefest weekend for an apple butter-making demonstration, live music, and apple dumplings.

TASTE OF THE REGION

KANSAS CITY BARBECUE

Pitmasters in Kansas City, 40 minutes from Weston, will typically slow-smoke cuts of dry-rubbed pork, beef, or chicken with hickory wood to infuse the meats with a distinct smoky flavor. Kansas City barbecue sauce is sweet and thick, usually made with a base of ketchup and/or tomato sauce, molasses, and brown sugar. American chef and restaurateur Henry Perry is credited with starting the Kansas City barbecue craze in the early 1920s. Today, people travel from around the world to get a taste of this distinctive culinary culture.

Weston Bend State Park is full of natural beauty and state history, such as this old tobacco barn.

Main Street, Pirtle Winery is housed in a historic Lutheran Evangelical church from 1867. Missouri law states that a winery cannot be built within 100 feet of a church, so the winemakers at Pirtle just converted the whole building. That cheeky spirit comes through in its refreshing, award-winning, fruit-forward wines, which can be sipped in the vine-covered garden tucked next to the winery.

The world-class National Silk Art Museum, in the former Bank of Weston building, displays the world's largest collection of woven silk tapestries made on punch-card mechanical looms. Rotating exhibits showcase French, German, Spanish, and English weaving—a collective tapestry of history. See hundreds of masterworks in up-close displays and learn how the mechanical loom influenced the birth of modern computing and data storage.

For a town of less than 2,000 people, Weston has a surprising number of boutique hotels and B&Bs. The Weston Steamboat Inn, set in the home of a former riverboat captain, pays homage to the area's boating history. Rooms feature beautiful claw-foot tubs, and the grounds have inviting firepits alongside the lush gardens. The Hatchery House Bed and Breakfast, a block off Main Street, is directly across from O'Malley's 1842 Pub, a speakeasy that serves hearty Irish food and has live music on weekends. The Tin Kitchen, operating out of an 1840s hardware store, serves pecan-wood-smoked meats under an original tin ceiling.

Delicious-Refreshing.
DRINK
Coca-Cola

NEBRASKA CITY

NEBRASKA

Nebraska City sits along the curving banks of the Missouri River right on the Nebraska-Iowa border, less than an hour south of Omaha. Historic buildings painted with vintage advertising and murals line Central Avenue, along with cottonwood, hackberry, American basswood, and downy hawthorn trees.

Arbor Day has become synonymous with Nebraska City. After all, the town was home to J. Sterling Morton, who founded the holiday in 1872. Initially, Morton encouraged Nebraskans to plant trees to protect crops from erosion and create an effective windbreak—the trees also provided fuel and shade to the community. An estimated one million trees were planted in Nebraska on that first Arbor Day; by 1920, more than 45 states were celebrating the holiday. The occasion became a national holiday in 1970. And today, planting trees represents something bigger. In Nebraska City, the Arbor Day Festival still brings community members together every spring to plant a tree for the good of the future. Visit during the festival to participate in the tree planting and enjoy community bar nights, local vendor pop-ups, a 10k (or 5k) fun run, and free admission to certain museums and historic sites around town.

The Lied Lodge on Nebraska City's Arbor Day Farm is a gorgeous Adirondack-style hotel overlooking lush green treetops and a campus full of history, trails, and apple-picking opportunities. The farm encompasses 260 acres, but a short, scenic

Nebraska City celebrates the fall season with the AppleJack Festival and parade in September. Early birds get the best spots.

ADVENTURE ALONG THE WAY

CARHENGE

Great Britain may have Stonehenge, but Alliance, Nebraska—seven hours west of Nebraska City—has Carhenge. Artist Jim Reinders built Carhenge in 1987 after studying the design and purpose of Stonehenge. For his version, he placed 39 cars in a replica of the ancient stones and sprayed them with gray paint. Sunset is the best time for viewing Carhenge. Be sure to stop in at the Pit Stop Gift Shop for quirky memorabilia.

Arbor Day Farm features apple orchards, hiking trails, and Treetop Village, with 11 interconnected tree houses.

walk through the trees on Doug's Trail takes guests from the hotel to Arbor Lodge State Historical Park, which was bequeathed to Nebraska by the Morton family in the 1920s. Here, visitors can tour the family's stately 52-room mansion, which has loads of historical artifacts, as well as the grounds, which are filled with lilac bushes, gardens, and trails.

You'll also want to visit the Tree Adventure at Arbor Day Farm. The farm's Treetop Village is a series of 11 tree houses connected by bridges and netted walkways. After exploring, enjoy locally made goods such as pies, jams, popcorn, and apple cider slushies at the Apple House Market. The Lied Greenhouse educates visitors on how trees are grown on the farm, and the orchard has more than two dozen varieties of apple trees. The price of admission helps support the tree-planting mission of the Arbor Day Foundation. You can also take home a small tree sapling, a living memory of Nebraska City.

Culinary-minded visitors should come in the fall for the AppleJack Festival; it's the best time of year to try a crisp apple (or an apple crisp). About five minutes northwest of town is Kimmel Orchard and Vineyard. Here, rows of apple trees stretch across 40 acres and entice with the opportunity to pick your own bushel. Cidermaking demonstrations are held in the Apple Barn during the fall, and the sweet, tart apple cider is just one of the many treats available for purchase.

GARRISON

NORTH DAKOTA

A colorful 26-foot-tall statue of Wally the Walleye stands proudly above the Garrison welcome sign—fitting considering that this small town is the walleye capital of the world. Visit Garrison and Lake Sakakawea State Park for a summer-weekend getaway filled with fishing, hiking, and pontoon boating along the south shore of the third largest human-made reservoir in the country. Along with walleye, northern pike and Chinook salmon fill Lake Sakakawea. Grasslands and prairies stretch around the lake as far as the eye can see. Visit in August to see the fields come alive with brilliant yellow sunflowers.

For hiking and mountain biking, check out the Nux Baa Gaa Trail, which begins at the Indian Hills Campground. Hikes like Whitetail Run and the Sakakawea Trail, part of the Lewis and Clark Legacy Trail system, wind through the hills behind Lake Sakakawea.

Lake Sakakawea State Park offers year-round fishing access, including ice fishing in winter. The lake is home to salmon, walleye, bass, and northern pike.

If Ye Olde Malt Shoppe on Garrison's Main Street doesn't completely satisfy your small-town nostalgia bug with its more than 18 flavors of ice cream (such as butter brickle, lemon bar, and huckleberry), numerous local festivals will. Sky Fest Over Fort Stevenson is an annual kite festival in May that continues a tradition started by residents in 1992. In August, the Aw Shucks! Corn Fest offers live music and free corn on the cob, plus numerous local vendors selling other tasty treats and wares. Garrison is a place to slow down and enjoy the surrounding beauty and a palpable sense of community.

ADVENTURE ALONG THE WAY

WORLD'S LARGEST BUFFALO

In Jamestown, North Dakota—two and a half hours southeast of Garrison—stands the world's largest buffalo. In 1959, sculptor Elmer Petersen created "Dakota Thunder," a 26-foot-tall concrete statue weighing 60 tons. The buffalo was christened in a statewide naming contest in 2010 and has gone on to become one of the most popular roadside attractions in the Midwest.

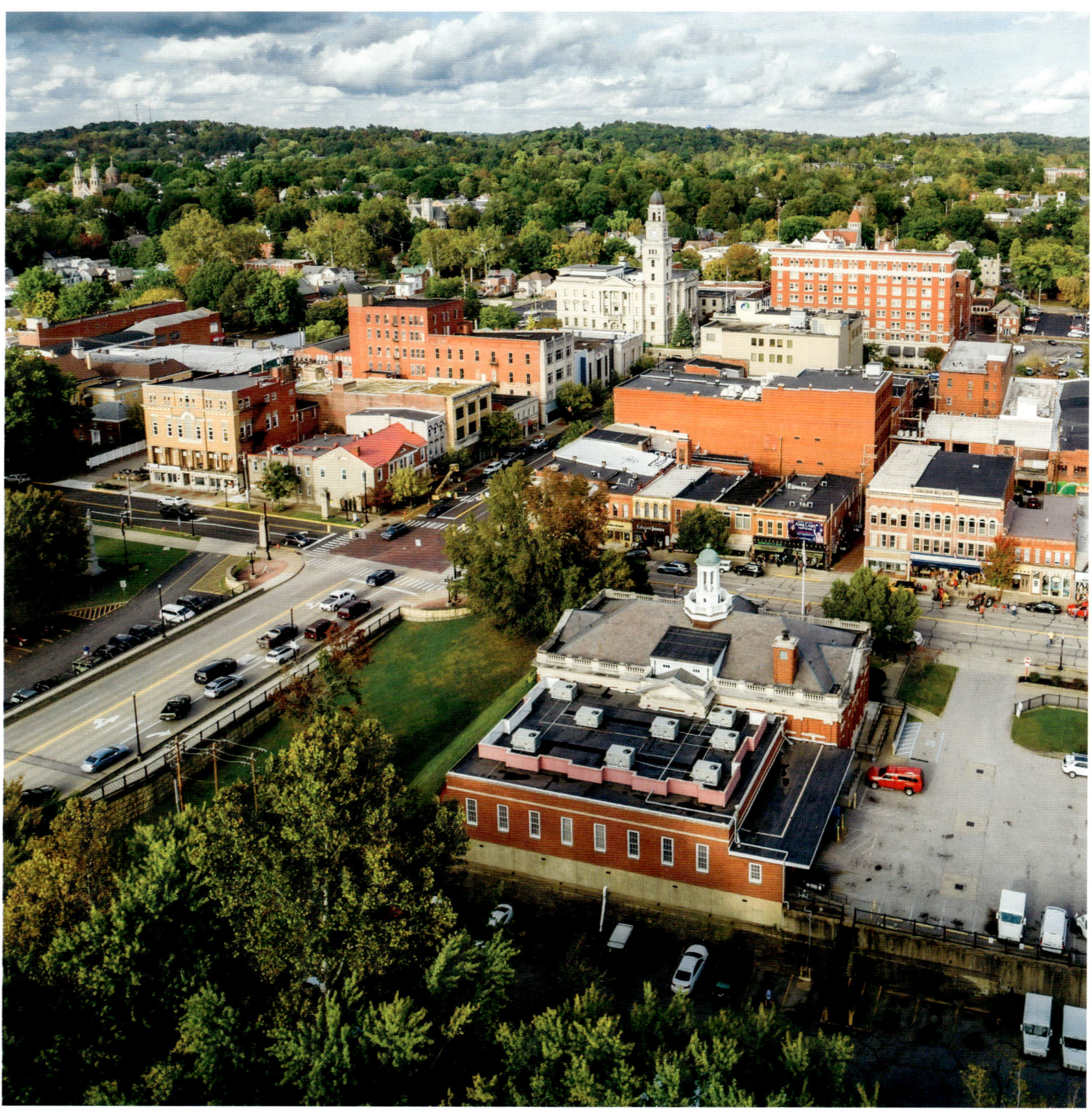

MARIETTA

OHIO

The two best ways to explore the river town of Marietta are by stern-wheeler along the river or by trolley tour through the historic downtown. Stretched alongside the confluence of the Ohio and Muskingum Rivers, Marietta was founded in 1788 as the first permanent settlement in the Northwest Territory and was a catalyst for the United States' northwestern expansion. Its name was chosen in honor of Marie Antoinette, as a sign of gratitude for France's aide in victory during the Revolutionary War.

History greets visitors at every turn in Marietta. The Campus Martius Museum is on the site of the original stockade of the Ohio Company (a colonial group founded to trade with Native Americans while also laying English claim to the Ohio River Valley) and includes the restored Rufus Putnam House, which showcases the lives of the earliest settlers in the area. The annual Ohio River Sternwheel Festival celebrates the inland waterways with a weekend of fireworks and paddle wheelers each September.

Marietta Trolley Tours offers expert-led trolley rides past landmarks throughout town. The stately brick Betsey Mills Club was founded in 1911 to help young women transition from farm to city life, and operates today with a community-centered approach. The spires of the Castle, an 1855 Gothic Revival-style home, stretch toward the sky from a beautifully manicured, tree-filled lawn. The Mound

Marietta's city center is charming year-round, but visit May to September, when hundreds of downtown lampposts are outfitted with baskets of fresh flowers, for a real treat.

TASTE OF THE REGION

BUCKEYE CANDY

Named for the Ohio-native buckeye tree and crafted to look similar to the buckeye nut, this candy treat is a delicious peanut butter ball dipped in dark chocolate. Invented in 1919 by the wives of the owner and salesmen of the Buckeye Candy Company, these treats are especially popular with Ohio State University Buckeye football fans, who think of the confection as a good luck charm.

JustAJar Design Press on Front Street, run by a husband-and-wife team, produces art for many local businesses and events.

Cemetery serves as a final resting spot for many Revolutionary War officers and is home to the Great Mound, or Conus, a prehistoric Adena burial mound that is believed to date back to between 100 B.C. and A.D. 500.

Colorful flower boxes and vintage murals line the brick facades of Front Street, Marietta's main thoroughfare. Historic buildings have been populated anew with a charming collection of boutiques and restaurants. Listen for the soft whirring of the antique printing press at JustAJar Design Press, which creates custom woodcut and letterpress posters. The Cook's Shop offers gorgeous home goods and kitchenware. And Wit and Whimzy sells unique goods and gifts crafted by small makers from Ohio and surrounding states. Much of Marietta's historic downtown is a designated outdoor refreshment area, which means that Wednesday through Saturday, locals and tourists can stroll through the streets with a cocktail in hand.

Originally built in 1859, Historic Harmar Bridge is the only remaining hand-turned swing railroad bridge in the country—though you can no longer walk or drive across it while it goes through rehabilitation. The Putnam Bridge (also known as the Marietta Bridge) takes you over the Muskingum River to reach the Harmar Village neighborhood. Here, museums and quirky shops are housed in buildings listed on the National Register of Historic Places. Passiflora Studio is a stunning flower boutique that

MARIETTA
OHIO
STERNWHEELIN'
BIKE RIDIN'
BOAT PADDLIN'
MOUND BUILDIN'
PAWPAW EATIN'
HISTORY HONORIN'
PIONEERIN'
GOOD TIMIN'
COMMUNITY
CARVING BLOCKS
HOBO
TAKE ME TO THE RIVER

OPPOSITE TOP: The Ohio River Sternwheel Festival climaxes with a fireworks display. OPPOSITE BOTTOM: The National Memorial to the "Start Westward of the United States" stands in Muskingum Park. LEFT: Spot Passiflora Studio's eye-catching facade in the Harmar Village neighborhood.

sells hand-tied bouquets from a vintage bike cart on Flower Bike Fridays. Every July, the neighborhood hosts the Harmar Days Festival, which raises funds to help restore and maintain the Harmar Bridge. Climb up to the lookout on Harmar Hill to see the city lights across the Muskingum River.

The Ohio River Museum in downtown Marietta offers tours of the *W. P. Snyder Jr.,* the last intact steam-powered stern-wheeler towboat in the United States. Life on the river today takes a more recreational pace. Nothing beats a sunset cruise on the deck of a stern-wheeler around Marietta.

ADVENTURE ALONG THE WAY

NEWARK EARTHWORKS

The largest set of geometric earthen enclosures in the world can be found near the Ohio towns of Newark and Heath, each less than a two-hour drive from Marietta. These incredibly preserved complexes were made by Indigenous peoples more than 2,000 years ago. Newark Earthworks was a sacred gathering space for Indigenous tribes to practice spiritual traditions and is considered an architectural wonder of ancient America. Today, three portions are preserved: the Great Circle, encompassing 30 acres of land; the Wright Square, a small section of earthwork; and the Octagon, a combined circle and octagon spanning about 70 acres.

MARCO DE OHIO
243
OHIO SILVER CO
245
SALE
OPEN
FRI 7
SAT 7

YELLOW SPRINGS

OHIO

This small hippie town encourages you to come as you are and to do your own thing. About 30 minutes east of Dayton, Yellow Springs' colorful downtown holds funky murals, sculptures, and art installations around every corner, as well as an eclectic mix of galleries, boutiques, and restaurants. A walk down Xenia Avenue will lead to encounters with buskers performing on stoops and street corners. Everyone is welcome here.

Yellow Springs was founded in 1825 by families wanting to create a socialist utopia. Though that vision never fully manifested, a pervasive commitment to social justice and equality remains present today. Yellow Springs was one of the final stops on the Underground Railroad, and in 1979 it became the smallest municipality to pass legislation protecting LGBTQIA+ rights.

Start your exploration of the area on the Little Miami Scenic Trail, which stretches more than 78 miles and was one of the first rail-to-trail projects in the country. A canopy of hickory, pawpaw, and redbud trees provides a shady respite during hot summer days, making it a perfect spot for a jog or bike ride. Adjacent to the trail is dog-friendly Yellow Springs Brewery, where you can rest your feet and enjoy a hoppy Boat Show IPA. Or, shortly after the trail crosses Yellow Springs Creek, take an offshoot

Muralist Pierre Nagley honored a late Yellow Springs resident with this artwork on the wall of the Ohio Silver Company.

ADVENTURE ALONG THE WAY

GLEN HELEN NATURE PRESERVE

If you're curious how the town of Yellow Springs got its name, look no further than Glen Helen Nature Preserve, just east of town. A winding trail through a deciduous forest leads to a small spring with a unique rusty yellow hue—due to high levels of iron in the water—that led to its name. Farther in the park is the Cascades, a beautiful waterfall stemming from Birch Creek. You'll also find the Glen Helen Raptor Center, a nonprofit dedicated to conservation and rehabilitation of injured raptors across southwestern Ohio. The owl named Daisy Duck is a particularly friendly ambassador.

Spot this double waterfall in Clifton Gorge State Nature Preserve.

trail north and lay out a picnic at Ellis Pond. The tranquil setting is a birder's paradise. Bird-watchers have reported sighting at least 75 species here since 2008.

At Clifton Gorge State Nature Preserve, limestone and dolomite gorges squeeze the rushing waters of the Little Miami River into a spot called the Narrows. Light streams through the vibrantly green trees along the park's hiking trails, one of which leads to the historic 19th-century Clifton Mill, among the largest water-powered gristmills still operating. Enjoy breakfast here—it's served all day—with the sounds of water tumbling from the mill into the river below.

In September, sunflower fields bloom for miles surrounding Yellow Springs. Come spring, Village Flower Farm offers pick-your-own daffodils and tulips. Young's Jersey Dairy, a staple in Yellow Springs since 1869, is famous for its Jersey dairy cows and farm-fresh ice cream. Check out its "cowlendar" of events for family-friendly activities throughout the year, including a corn maze in summer and a pumpkin patch in fall.

Find top-notch entertainment at YS Firehouse, a comedy club opened by comedian Dave Chappelle in a former fire station just off the Little Miami Scenic Trail. Intimate comedy shows, film screenings, and live music performances play to sold-out crowds. Movie lovers should visit in October for the Yellow Springs Film Festival, hosted in part by the local, independent Little Art Theatre.

ORIGINAL LOCATION OF SALOON No 10
HISTORIC SPOT OF THE OLD WEST 1876
624
OPEN
Seth Bullock
SHERIFF
Deadwood
Dakota
Territory
WILD BILL
BAR
PATRIOT WHISKEY
BUY - SELL - TRADE
GUNS
GAMBLING
ANTIQUES
COWBOY WESTERN
HISTORIC ITEMS

DEADWOOD

SOUTH DAKOTA

The entire town of Deadwood is a designated national historic landmark. Wild West and gold-mining history pervades the town's restaurants and saloons, especially during the daily shootout reenactments held in the late afternoon and early evening. Mount Moriah Cemetery, the final resting place for many Western icons, including Wild Bill himself, sits on a steep ravine. Visitors leave decks of cards, cash, and packs of cigarettes on the famous grave. Museums throughout town, such as the Adams Museum, the Brothel, and the Days of '76 Museum, provide integral narratives of Deadwood and the region's unique pioneer past. And in a fitting link between past and present, much of the money used for historical preservation has come courtesy of revenue from limited-stakes gaming, which was made legal here in 1989. To date, the town has collected more than $200 million from gambling—and its authenticity has slowly but surely been restored.

Deadwood still commemorates Saloon No. 10, where, in 1876, an assassin shot Wild Bill Hickok.

Deadwood is nestled in Black Hills National Forest. Named Paha Sapa ("hills that are black") by the native Lakota people for the shadowy cast of ponderosa pine trees on the landscape's granite formations, the hills shift into brilliant hues of green, red, brown, and gold, depending on how the sunlight hits. Black Elk Peak, the highest point east of the Rocky Mountains, provides hikers with panoramic vistas of craggy rocks, rolling hills, and lush vegetation. Take a route to the summit past the crystal waters of Sylvan Lake. Close by is the big draw: Mount Rushmore. More than two million people visit the iconic landmark

TALK LIKE A LOCAL

"DEADMAN'S HAND"

When Wild Bill Hickok was shot dead in Saloon No. 10 by Jack McCall, he was playing poker and, according to legend, holding a pair of aces and a pair of eights. Today, that particular grouping of cards is known as the "deadman's hand." Two pairs will win you a few hands in poker, but beware opponents with three of a kind (or nasty tempers).

Paddleboard, kayak, canoe, and fish on Silver Lake in Custer State Park, encompassing 71,000 acres in the Black Hills.

each year. Another nearby stone carving (still in progress) is the Crazy Horse Memorial, depicting the Oglala Lakota warrior sculpted into Thunderhead Mountain.

The 109-mile George S. Mickelson Trail runs north-south through the Black Hills. The trailhead starts in Deadwood and winds through rock tunnels, past spruce and ponderosa pine forests, and over more than 100 converted railroad bridges. Biking the trail will provide a beautiful adventure.

For those looking for a less strenuous way to take in the wilderness, drive the Wildlife Loop Road in Custer State Park. The winding route through breezy grasslands and tree-covered hills is best enjoyed at half speed to glimpse wild bison, bighorn sheep, pronghorn, and a host of native birds.

ADVENTURE ALONG THE WAY

CORN PALACE

Mitchell, South Dakota, about four and a half hours east of Deadwood, is home to an Americana folk-art wonder. The self-proclaimed World's Only Corn Palace, established in 1892, is a multipurpose arena that's decorated annually with natural-colored corn, among other native grasses and grains, for the Corn Palace Festival, held every August. Throughout the rest of the year, the Corn Palace hosts dances, stage shows, banquets, and regional and state basketball games, among other events. The arena attracts more than 500,000 visitors each year, with a peak during the beloved August festival.

CEDARBURG

WISCONSIN

Just 20 minutes north of Milwaukee is the quiet town of Cedarburg, where stately white cedars, elms, and paper birch trees form something of an urban forest along streets filled with unique shops. This is a welcoming place to explore the unique shops and boutiques in town. The trailhead to the 30-mile paved Ozaukee Interurban Trail begins nearby, connecting towns throughout Ozaukee County along the original route of the Interurban Electric Railway. A designated Great Wisconsin Birding and Nature Trail, the paved trail gives bike riders and hikers an opportunity to take in the beauty of the region.

European immigrants, mostly German and Irish, arrived here in the early 1840s and built gristmills and woolen mills that eventually supplied textiles to the Civil War effort. The mill town's transformation into modern-day Cedarburg was spurred by a creativity-centered preservationist attitude. The Wisconsin Museum of Quilt and Fiber Arts showcases masterpieces in a rustic restored 1850s barn. The Cedarburg Art Museum on Washington Avenue is located in a redbrick Victorian and features a summer beer garden on its back patio, which is fitting since beer, history, and the arts go hand in hand here. After a museum stop, pop in for a drink at Anvil Pub, in an old blacksmith shop, or Rebellion Brewing, which sits along Cedar Creek on the first floor of the historic limestone Cedarburg Mill.

Time your trip to coincide with one of Cedarburg's many festivals. The Giant Pumpkin Charity Regatta, held as part of the annual Cedarburg Wine and Harvest Festival each September, is unlike anything else in the country. Teams paddle, push, and pull hollowed-out 600-pound pumpkins across Cedar Creek in a crowd-pleasing race. June is the height of berry season and brings with it the highly anticipated Cedarburg Strawberry Festival, one of four annual town festivals that showcase the beauty of the city, encourage tourism, and bring the local community together.

Seasonal festivals take place year-round in Cedarburg. Align your trip with the Strawberry Festival, Wine and Harvest Festival, Oktoberfest, Winter Festival, or Maxwell Street Days.

EGG HARBOR

WISCONSIN

Come summer, families from all over Wisconsin head north to Door County on the peninsula between Lake Michigan and Green Bay. Many head to Egg Harbor, one of the county's most charming towns, with a lovely balance of outdoor offerings and a thriving arts and music scene. It's also possibly one of the only towns in the country allegedly named after a food fight.

As the story goes, on June 23, 1825, a legendary egg battle took place. As early fur traders raced one another to shore, they began pelting each other with eggs. The fun continued the next day until the sandy beach was littered with eggshells—and so Egg Harbor was christened. Though others say that the name came from a nest of eggs found near the shore, most prefer the jovial egg-fight version.

Hop on a complimentary turquoise Eggy bike to explore town and see resident artists at work in their studios among bustling galleries. Off the Wheel Pottery, housed in an old timber-framed barn and granary, features nature-inspired works by Reneé Schwaller as well as from potters from around the country. Plum Bottom Gallery has a unique, carefully curated collection of handcrafted pieces in all art mediums for you to browse or take home.

It's not a visit to Wisconsin without cheese. Wisconsin Cheese Masters sells state originals including a rustic Mobay; a nutty, caramelly Cardona; and an alpine-style Grand Cru Surchoix. Join their Cheese of the Month Club for shipments of specialty cheeses curated by the masters for when you have a hankering back at home. Pair your favorite

Harbor View Park is a great spot to have a picnic, take a stroll, or watch the sun set over Green Bay Harbor.

ADVENTURE ALONG THE WAY

MARS' CHEESE CASTLE

On the drive north from Milwaukee to Egg Harbor you'll pass the Mars' Cheese Castle, in the town of Kenosha. It has been a purveyor of the state's culinary icons for more than six decades, so this is a must-stop for sampling Wisconsin's best, including cheese curds, cheese logs, cheese spreads, and cheese-flavored popcorn. Grab a King's Ransom box for a selection of its best sellers.

Spring brings cherry blossoms to Egg Harbor's orchards. Peak bloom period is mid-May.

cheeses with freshly baked bread from MacReady Artisan Bread Company; don't miss the Door County tart cherry and dried cranberry bread, which mixes regional flavors together.

The smooth waters of Green Bay off Egg Harbor Beach beckon paddleboarders and swimmers. Paddle out in a kayak for spectacular sunset views. Summer concerts are also a must. Park yourself among the folding chairs and picnics on the Egg Harbor Amphitheater's lawn for the free evening concert series. Watch the vibrant sunset over the harbor and enjoy a glass of local wine while listening to live tunes. Or take in a set at the Concerts in the Park series at Harbor View Park, where neighbors and visitors alike gather, contributing to the welcoming community vibe throughout Egg Harbor.

Lush fields surround the charming red barn turned cider mill at Lautenbach's Orchard Country, a 10-minute drive north of town. Springtime at the orchards brings a bountiful array of blooms, with cherry blossoms popping in the middle of May and apple blossoms about a week later. Summer Cherry Fest at Lautenbach's is an especially delightful time to visit; the delicious smell of freshly baked cherry doughnuts wafts across the rolling hillside as folks meander through the orchard picking cherries right off the trees and enjoying live music. Don't miss out on the cherry-pit spitting contest. To bring a taste of Door County home, pick up one of the orchard's award-winning fruit-forward wines or ciders.

CHEESE
Wisconsin
CHEESE
Masters
OPEN

OUR FAMOUS
CHERRY $12
CRANBERRY

OPPOSITE TOP: Pad your travel budget for a visit to Wisconsin Cheese Masters. OPPOSITE BOTTOM: Cherry-cranberry bread awaits you at MacReady Artisan Bread Company. LEFT: Take home a piece from Off the Wheel Pottery.

Harbor Ridge Winery, just a mile from downtown, is an excellent spot to sip, shop, and linger awhile. Their cherry wine, a traditional sweet varietal is a must-try, but don't skip the creative blends like Two Rows Make a White, a blend of Vidal blanc and gewürztraminer, or the cheekily named Gimme One Good Riesling and Knockin' Heads Red. The log cabin tasting room opens onto a patio made for temperate afternoons. Visit on a weekend to enjoy live music. Harbor Ridge is another stop on the Door Country Trolley wine tour, which takes wine enthusiasts to three wineries in a bright red old-fashioned trolley bus. If you're looking for something different, Door County Trolley also runs ghost tours, lighthouse tours, and family-friendly tours that stop in and around Egg Harbor.

TASTE OF THE REGION

BOOYAH STEW

Booyah stew is a hearty dish often served at tailgates and potlucks in the Green Bay area. Ingredients include several types of meat (such as chicken, beef, and sometimes pork), potatoes, and tons of vegetables, such as cabbage, tomatoes, onions, carrots, and celery. Though it's traditionally slow-cooked in a large cast-iron kettle over an open flame, a Dutch oven on the stovetop will do just fine. For a finishing touch, top your stew with oyster crackers.

LAKE GENEVA

WISCONSIN

An enigmatic spirit lives along the lakeshore of a small Wisconsin town. Big Foot, the legendary chief of the Potawatomi people (not the mythical beast), was said to have earned his name for the massive snowshoe footprints he left on the area's powdery winter hillsides. Chief Big Foot's love of nature and peace continues to influence the community-minded focus of Lake Geneva—just a short drive from both Chicago and Milwaukee—today.

The Lake Geneva Shore Path marries natural beauty with human-made splendor and is a great introduction to the town. It was carved out by the Potawatomi thousands of years ago to connect villages around the lake. Today, you can follow the nearly 22-mile pathway along the wooded shoreline to see sailboats gliding in the clear blue waters and magnificent Gilded Age lakefront estates, historic summer homes of the Chicago elite that were built between the late 1800s and early 1900s.

Visitors can enjoy Geneva Lake via a rented sailboat or pontoon or take a guided tour. Soak in the views at sunset.

Each section of the shore path is maintained by individual estate owners, creating a varied walkway with unique stonework, fluffy hydrangeas, colorful coneflowers, and even a "magic mailbox" with a guestbook for hikers to sign.

Each estate is impressive in its own right. Stone Manor is the largest lakefront property, built in 1899; its Bedford limestone exterior rises impressively from a rolling green hillside. Hillcroft, a cottage-style hunting lodge, once belonged to the Wrigley

TALK LIKE A LOCAL

"BUBBLER"

Don't ask a Wisconsinite for the location of a water fountain. In this state, it's a bubbler, named, as the story goes, for a product invented in 1888 by the Wisconsin-based Kohler Company. (An original Kohler bubbler sits immortalized in Madison, an hour and a half from Lake Geneva.) The initial bubbler got its name from the bubble effect it created when it shot water one inch straight into the air. Though the machine was later redesigned to shoot the water in an arc for easier drinking, the name stuck—at least in Wisconsin.

Stone Manor was built in 1899.

family of chewing gum fame. Then there is the white-columned Driehaus Estate and Glanworth Gardens, a Georgian-style construction built in 1906 and meticulously landscaped by Frederick Law Olmsted, the famed designer of New York's Central Park.

For outdoor enthusiasts, an afternoon at the beach or on one of the excellent golf courses in Lake Geneva is a day well spent. The northern shoreline at Big Foot Beach State Park is a family-friendly spot with clear waters beckoning swimmers and paddlers alike. Sunsets are best observed with a cocktail at the quirky Popeye's on Lake Geneva (not to be confused with the fast-food chain) or over an elegant meal at the Grandview Restaurant. Riviera Beach, just off the Short Path, is close to downtown and easy to find: Just look for its bright umbrellas. Geneva National Resort and Club has 54 holes designed by golf legends Arnold Palmer, Gary Player, and Lee Trevino. Numerous greens back right up to the lake for the ultimate scenic round.

TASTE OF THE REGION

CHEESE CURDS

A fresh Wisconsin cheese curd will make a distinctive squeak when you bite into it—a sound that means it's fresh. Wisconsinites debate whether this local delicacy is best served fried or raw, but either way the morsel is celebrated on National Cheese Curd Day every October. Eat the curds plain, piled atop fries and smothered in gravy, or fried with spicy ranch dip.

PART FIVE

WEST AND PACIFIC NORTHWEST

The Three Sisters mountains will be the backdrop of almost any photograph in Sisters, Oregon (page 368).

OPEN
19815

SITKA

ALASKA

You can reach Sitka only by air or water. Thanks to its remote setting and natural environment in southeastern Alaska, wilderness and culture coalesce in a unique community here. Tlingit people inhabited Sitka for more than 10,000 years, until Russians claimed the land in 1808 and called it New Archangel. The Russian influence is obvious in the town's architecture, including the onion-shaped domes of St. Michael's Cathedral, the first Russian Orthodox cathedral built in North America, which was added to the National Register of Historic Places in 1966. The United States took over after the 1867 Alaska Purchase, which was marked by the official transfer ceremony on top of Sitka's Castle Hill, also known as Baranof Castle State Historic Site, now a national historic landmark. The site represents the convergence of Tlingit, Russian, and American history and rises above the town center with incredible views of Sitka Harbor.

The Sitka Channel funnels the local fishing industry through the rest of the community.

A mile east at Sitka National Historical Park, accessible hiking trails wind through a forest, passing more than 20 historic totem poles. The park commemorates the 1804 Battle of Sitka, in which Indigenous Tlingit fought Russian traders for control of the land. The totem poles, carved by Tlingit and Haida artists, were collected and placed in 1906 and convey the ancestry, folklore, or history of a particular clan, or commemorate a person of note. See them all on the Totem Trail, an easy one-mile loop. For a more immersive Indigenous cultural experience, spend an evening

TALK LIKE A LOCAL

"BREAKUP SEASON"

Alaskans refer to the shoulder season—the end of winter when the ice on mountains and river drifts begins to break apart—as "breakup season." Along with the physical breaking apart of the ice, it also signifies it's time for residents to "break up" with their favorite winter activities, like skiing, snowshoeing, and ice skating.

The Sheet'ká Kwáan Naa Kahídi Community House hosts special performances of Tlingit dances. The traditional robes in this image took more than a year to weave.

at the Sheet'ká Kwáan Naa Kahídi Community House to watch dancers perform Tlingit songs and dances.

Life around and in the water is a critical part of Sitka's culture. Gentle marine giants like gray whales, humpback whales, orcas, and porpoises live in the calm waters of Sitka Sound. Honor this natural world at WhaleFest in November, which celebrates the harmony between Sitkans, visitors, and the Alaska wilderness. To protect the water's wildlife, sustainable fishing has always been important in Sitka. Salmon, trout, char, and steelhead thrive in Sitka's fresh waters. During salmon-spawning season (summer and early fall) spot salmon running through Kaasda Héen, aka the Indian River. Those looking for saltwater sportfishing and fly-fishing opportunities will find plenty of responsible outfitters to suit their needs.

For additional outdoor adventures, hikers can walk along the Kaasda Héen Trail through Tongass National Forest to glimpse the Three Sisters mountains, and kayakers can paddle the wild coast to watch bald eagles swoop down from towering coastal spruce and hemlock trees to snatch fish. Take flight in a seaplane to circle remote mountain glaciers and grab an aerial view of the Mount Edgecumbe volcano, which has not had a major eruption in 4,000 years. Or visit the brown bears at Fortress of the Bear, a rescue center that takes in orphaned bears from all over the state.

OPPOSITE TOP: Tour Tlingit historic sites in Sitka National Historical Park. **OPPOSITE BOTTOM:** A pod of humpback whales feed in Sitka Sound. **LEFT:** St. Michael's Cathedral National Historic Landmark exemplifies Russia's past influence in North America.

Downtown Sitka is romantic and inspiring, so it's no wonder it was featured in the 2009 film *The Proposal,* starring Sandra Bullock and Ryan Reynolds. Pop into the Cellar for unique Alaska wares and gifts, take a stained glass–making class at Forget Me Not, or visit Beak Restaurant for homemade cinnamon doughnuts at brunch and award-winning local cuisine, with a spotlight on seafood, at dinner. For a unique stay, book the Sitka Lighthouse, where you'll wake up surrounded by crystal blue water and 360-degree views of Sitka and the Eastern Channel in a luxuriously renovated 1983 lighthouse. On a clear night with dark skies, you may even be dazzled by the dancing greens and yellows of the northern lights.

TASTE OF THE REGION

AKUTAQ

Made from reindeer fat, seal oil, fresh snow, wild berries, and occasionally ground fish, akutaq is an Alaska delicacy that Indigenous people have prepared and enjoyed for thousands of years. The name means "mix together" in Yupik. The berries used vary by region, but you'll find this celebratory dessert, which some refer to as "Eskimo ice cream," almost anywhere you go in Alaska.

NAGLEY'S STORE
SINCE 1921
TALKEETNA, ALASKA
WEST RIB
DELI & PUB
LIQUOR STORE
OPEN
PACKAGED ICE
CRYSTAL CLEAR ICE
ICE AXE

TALKEETNA

ALASKA

About two hours north of Anchorage sits the town of Talkeetna, an artsy mountain community and a perfect base for exploring Denali State Park, which offers the same jaw-dropping scenery as the national park of the same name two hours away—without the crowds. Talkeetna is unapologetically and authentically Alaska. The entire downtown was placed on the National Register of Historic Places to protect the railroad- and mining-era buildings of the early 1900s. Walk Main Street to find Nagley's Store, established around 1917 and still a local institution, and Wild Harvest, a shop that sells birch syrup, birch water, and wild chaga mushroom tea. Stop by Denali Brewpub for Alaska cod fish-and-chips and a pint, served with views of the vast mountains beyond.

During summer months, fish, hike, and take advantage of nearly 24 hours of daylight. (Most, if not all, lodging options will have blackout curtains for use during this time of year.) But those who brave the colder months can catch the iconic Iditarod Trail Sled Dog Race, held every March. At this world-famous event, mushers work with teams of 12 to 14 dogs to cover nearly 1,000 miles of Alaska wilderness, traversing mountain passes, rugged tundra, and sea ice. The race is regarded as a symbolic link to the early history of the state. Talkeetna Air Taxi offers "Chase the Race" aerial tours to watch the racers from above. Meanwhile, the Iditarod Museum is open year-round to experience the history of mushing.

Nagley's Store on Main Street, founded in 1921, sells coffee, sandwiches, sodas, and ice cream.

TASTE OF THE REGION

MOOSE'S TOOTH

Moose's Tooth is an Alaska institution and a must-stop on your way out of Anchorage for a piping-hot pizza and a cold six-pack of Broken Tooth beer. Moose's Tooth is named for the iconic rock peak in the Alaska Range. Founded in 1996 by a rock climber and home brewer, the restaurant is a beloved community gathering place.

AVALON

CALIFORNIA

What do you get when old Hollywood meets the Mediterranean? It might just be the quaint town of Avalon on Santa Catalina Island—the southernmost city in Los Angeles County. Pulling up to the harbor at Avalon Bay (the town is accessible only by ferry) in view of the white stucco buildings dotting the surrounding cliffs feels as if you've been transported onto a movie set. In fact, many classics of the silent-film era were filmed on the island, starring celebrities such as Charlie Chaplin, Joan Crawford, and Clark Gable. The Catalina Casino, built by the Wrigley family (of chewing gum fame) in 1929 and set high on a cliff looking over Descanso Beach and Avalon Bay, was an old-time hot spot. Today, it's a boutique movie theater and a beautiful example of art deco and Mediterranean Revival architecture.

Most Avalon residents and visitors get around by golf cart. Take one to zip over to Lover's Cove, a popular spot to snorkel, kayak, and paddleboard. The Garden to Sky Hike, which begins at the Wrigley Memorial and Botanic Garden, is another wonderful way to see the beauty of the island.

The annual Catalina Wine Mixer—yes, modeled after the iconic scene from the 2008 movie *Step Brothers*—in June is a fun beach-party festival that attracts a younger crowd looking for a weekend of sun, water, music, and wine. In contrast, May's Avalon Ball, hosted by the Art Deco Society of Los Angeles, is an elegant affair that celebrates the 1920s, complete with vintage costumes and big bands in the Avalon Casino.

The art-deco style Catalina Casino sits right on the water. Visitors can take a general-admission or VIP tour, or enjoy a flick at the boutique movie theater.

TASTE OF THE REGION

CALIFORNIA BURRITO

The California burrito, believed to have been invented in San Diego in the 1980s, is a unique mashup of Hispanic and California culinary influences. Ingredients include carne asada, rice, pico de gallo, french fries, cheese, sour cream, and guacamole. Decadent and satisfying, it is especially welcome after a big night on the town.

CARMEL-BY-THE-SEA

CALIFORNIA

Carmel-by-the-Sea's whimsical storybook architecture, hidden passageways, and tucked-away courtyards make it a must-visit destination. Situated in California's Central Coast region, the town was created in harmony with its natural environment. Upon its founding in 1902, the first order of business was planting 100 cypress trees in the barren coastal potato patches. As the town expanded, roads and businesses were often constructed around existing trees. Houses were built to a smaller scale and designed to blend in with the natural landscape, and artificial light, including streetlights, was restricted so that the moonlight off the ocean could shine.

The fairy-tale cottages the town is most famous for were the brainchild of Hugh Comstock, an American designer who went on to become a master builder. But before he reached that status, he built the renowned Hansel cottage for his wife's dollmaking business; the 1925 Gretel cottage is next door. In total, 21 of his fairy-tale cottages dot the town. Other artistic influences have made their mark, too. Clint Eastwood preserved and restored the historic 1800s Mission Ranch when he served as mayor here in the late 1980s. One of California's first dairies, the 22-acre ranch is now home to a 31-room inn, a restaurant and piano bar, and the Mission Ranch Tennis and Fitness Club. But it maintains its original character—and you can still watch sheep

Dogs frolic on Carmel Beach, where they're allowed off-leash. Downtown Carmel-by-the-Sea is dog friendly, too.

ADVENTURE ALONG THE WAY

BIG SUR

Big Sur, 40 minutes south of Carmel, is a popular hiking area with an extensive trail system through remote yet accessible wilderness. The Pacific Ocean and the Santa Lucia Mountains are unmatched in beauty and viewable from every route. For views of majestic McWay Falls pouring onto sandy McWay Cove, hike the short Waterfall Overlook Trail in Julia Pfeiffer Burns State Park. For a more strenuous path, Andrew Molera State Park has an eight-mile loop that winds along bluffs and ridges; it has great coastal views and beach access as well.

Architect Hugh Comstock's fairy-tale cottages have become emblematic of Carmel-by-the-Sea.

graze the grounds throughout the day. Frank Lloyd Wright's Mrs. Clinton (or Della) Walker House, known as the "Cabin on the Rocks," designed in 1948 and completed in 1951, juts out into the water from Carmel Point. The home was added to the National Register of Historic Places in 1977.

The overall impression of Carmel-by-the-Sea, or Carmel, is peaceful, serene, and laid-back. Folks take any chance to soak in the salty sea air, often with their dog by their side. In fact, Carmel is one of the easiest places in the United States to travel with your canine companion, and many tourism boards have rated it the most dog-friendly town in the United States. (There are 25 dog-friendly hotels and inns in town, and beaches and trails welcome dogs, too—just be mindful of leash laws.) This contributes to the pleasant atmosphere; it's quite common to see strangers chatting on the streets and welcoming tourists, often brought together by their dogs.

Walk down Ocean Avenue to explore Carmel's fantastic boutiques, local art galleries, and restaurants. The Cottage of Sweets is a traditional British-style treat shop offering delicious fudge and licorice candies both made in-store and imported. A few blocks away is Bud's bar, which celebrates Carmel's bohemian influences at its spot inside La Playa Hotel. About 10 minutes inland is Folktale Winery and Vineyard, an idyllic spot strewn with wildflowers and views of the Carmel River. Point Lobos State Natural Reserve offers stunning hikes, like the Bird

CARMEL
BAKERY
JEWELLERS
COCONUT MACAROON

OPPOSITE TOP: Carmel Bakery on Ocean Avenue offers European-style baked goods and pastries. **OPPOSITE BOTTOM:** Cypress trees populate Point Lobos State Natural Reserve. **LEFT:** Carmel Mission is an active parish, but visitors can tour the grounds, chapel, and museum outside of Mass hours.

Island Trail. And you can tour Carmel Mission, built in 1797 and otherwise known as Mission San Carlos Borroméo de Carmelo, the only Spanish mission in California with its original bell tower and bell still intact.

Between sunrise and sunset, take 17-Mile Drive along the coast for one of the most scenic drives in the world. Sights include dramatic cliffs, pure white beaches, and magical forests. The drive passes legendary Pebble Beach, a renowned public golf course that has hosted several major championships. If you're lucky enough to score an afternoon tee time, make sure to hang out at the clubhouse post-round. The bagpiper at Spanish Bay serenades golfers each day at sunset, backlit by the orange and red hues sinking into the breaking waves of the bay.

TASTE OF THE REGION

AVOCADO TOAST

The invention of avocado toast is hotly contested. Australians claim ownership of the dish, but Angelenos take credit for its popularity in the United States. Meanwhile, many from Cuba and Mexico point out they've been eating avocados and bread since ancient times. Whatever its origins, the dish is ubiquitous in the Golden State today.

HEALDSBURG

CALIFORNIA

While the town of Healdsburg has award-winning wineries, restaurants, and hotels, its laid-back atmosphere makes it an incredibly relaxing place. Healdsburg is set in the heart of Northern California's Sonoma County, along the Russian River. Start your visit in the 19th-century Healdsburg Plaza. Summer visitors can spread out picnic blankets for the Tuesday in the Plaza concert series or peruse one of the best farmers markets in California wine country. Little Saint is a funky arts-and-community complex where you can enjoy a plant-based meal, shop for wine, or grab a coffee. Noble Folk Ice Cream and Pie Bar is worth the wait in line to try artisanal sweet treats like a blood orange–raspberry baked custard pie.

Outside town, alternate between winery hopping and exploring pastoral California wine country. Riverfront Regional Park, on the Russian River, is a lovely area to hike, bike, or horseback ride around Lake Benoist and through a grove of coastal redwoods. The Russian River Valley American Viticultural Area is just one of three distinctive microclimates surrounding Healdsburg. Flowers Vineyard and Winery, known for exquisite pinot noir and chardonnay, has a beautiful tasting room surrounded by redwood groves and wildflower gardens. It's among the more than 80 vineyards you can sample from in this bucolic region. At Banshee in nearby Geyserville, spin a record and try the Bubbles and Caviar experience in the hipster-haven tasting room.

With local wines and food from any one of the area's farmers markets, a homegrown meal is easy to come by in Healdsburg.

ADVENTURE ALONG THE WAY

ARMSTRONG REDWOODS STATE NATURAL RESERVE

California's coastal redwoods are an indescribable natural treasure. The trees are the world's tallest living things and among its oldest, capable of surviving for thousands of years. A hike through Armstrong Redwoods State Natural Reserve is humbling and life-changing, and a reminder of the importance of our natural world.

PASO ROBLES

CALIFORNIA

Among the oak trees, olive groves, and vineyards on the southern end of California's Central Coast lies the small town of Paso Robles (pronounced ROH-bulz), which translates to "the pass of the oaks." In 1790, Franciscan friars introduced winemaking to Paso Robles, which was situated on the original King's Highway, or El Camino Real, a historic trail that is believed to have connected Spanish missions throughout California. The town is an incredible place to visit, filled with rich history and a year-round rotation of festivals and events, from Art in the Park in April and November to the Olive and Lavender Festival in May to the Firestone Walker Invitational Beer Fest in June. Balloons Over Paso is a hot-air balloon experience that offers riders an opportunity to appreciate the hills, vineyards, and oak groves with views from above.

Paso Robles is the Wild West of California wine, a region characterized by rule-breaking diversity and innovation. With more than 200 tasting rooms and 40,000 acres of vineyard to explore, it is the ideal place to experience new wineries and try lesser known varietals. The region is celebrated for cabernet sauvignon and Bordeaux-style blends; but other bold and rich wines like Syrah, Grenache-Syrah-Mourvèdre (GSM) blends, and Viognier also thrive in this warm climate adjacent to the Pacific

Heart Hill Vineyard in the Willow Creek District is so named for its iconic grove of oak trees, shaped in 1956.

ADVENTURE ALONG THE WAY

HEARST CASTLE

Hearst Castle (more formally called La Cuesta Encantada, or The Enchanted Hill), rises above the clouds on a hilltop overlooking San Simeon in San Luis Obispo County, an hour west of Paso Robles. Built between 1919 and 1947 by publishing tycoon William Randolph Hearst, and designed by architect Julia Morgan, the castle is now a historic house museum and California state park. The grandeur of this Mediterranean Revival-style estate is rivaled by the incomparable art collection inside. The opulence of a castle more commonly found in Europe is a true sight to behold in the California landscape.

Visit Fish Gaucho on Park Street for all manner of tacos, including short rib with tomatillo jam and Oaxaca cheese.

Ocean. Visit Daou Vineyards, perched on Daou Mountain in the hills of the Adelaida District, for stunning vistas and delicious tastings. For a craft experience, check out Brecon Estate, an award-winning small-batch winery with a casual, architecturally stunning tasting room and a patio tucked under oak trees. Tablas Creek Vineyard is the first Regenerative Organic Certified vineyard in the world (meaning it works to rehabilitate soil, protects animal welfare, and more) and was a pioneer of the California Rhône movement in the 1980s. Its tasting room is a beautiful place to spend an afternoon sampling wines that have been produced in the centuries-old Châteauneuf-du-Pape tradition of blending. Consider hiring a driver for the day or having a designated driver in your party, as the tasting rooms are spread throughout the hills and reception can be tricky in this rural area.

The focal point of Paso Robles is the sprawling five-acre Downtown City Park right in its center, filled with park benches and towering oak trees. The park is also the hosting ground of several Paso Robles happenings, including Pioneer Day, the Mid-State Fair Pancake Breakfast, and the annual Fourth of July celebration. Warm weather months also bring concerts in the park and a wine festival. Find an abundance of shops, restaurants, bars, and tasting rooms within walking distance of the park. Fish Gaucho is a favorite dinner spot for modern Mexican fare like short rib enchiladas and Wagyu tartare,

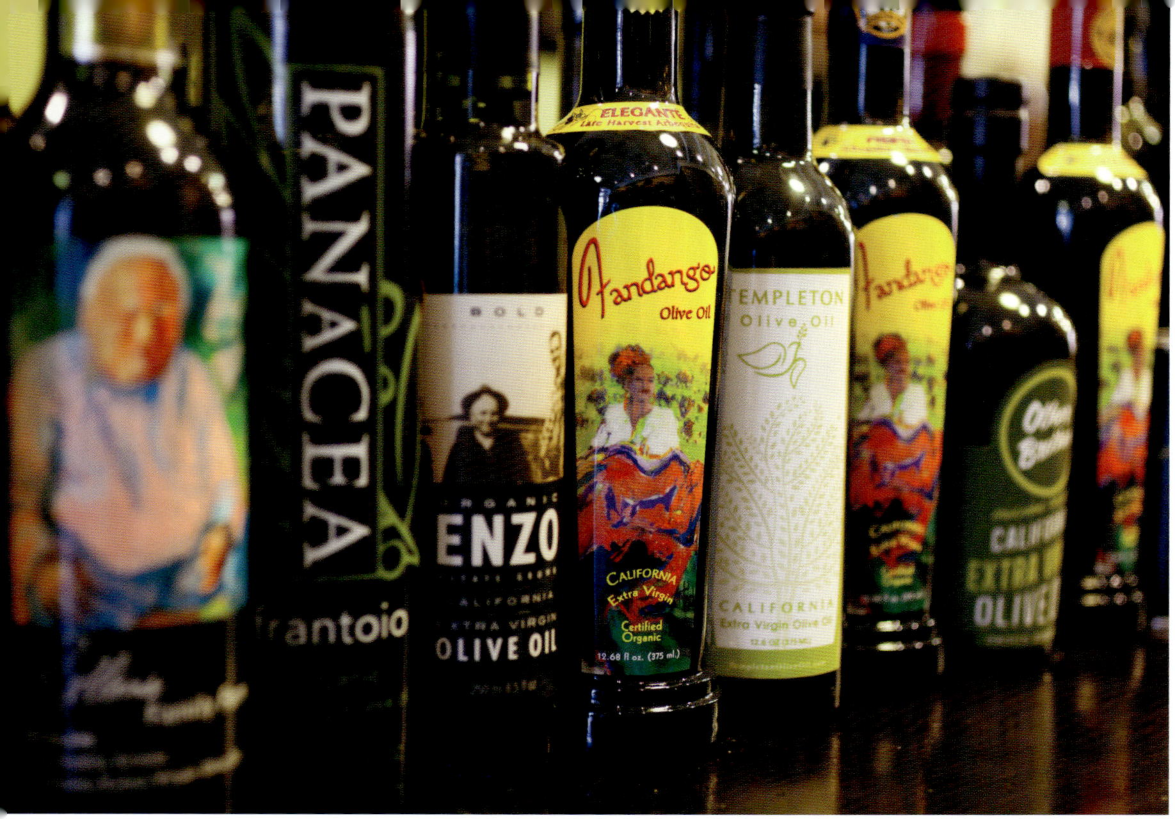
PANACEA
frantoio
BOLD
ENZO
CALIFORNIA
EXTRA VIRGIN
OLIVE OIL
ELEGANTE
Fandango
Olive Oil
CALIFORNIA
Extra Virgin
Certified Organic
12.68 fl oz. (375 ml.)
TEMPLETON
Olive Oil
CALIFORNIA
Extra Virgin Olive Oil

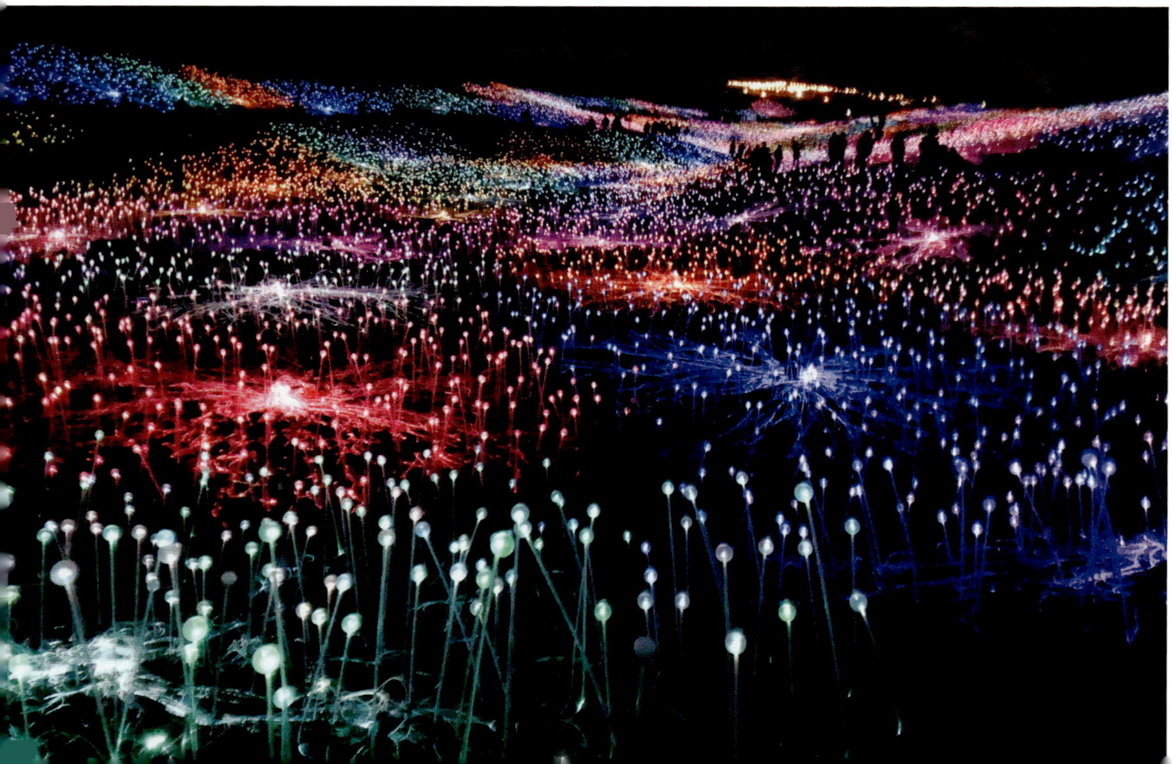

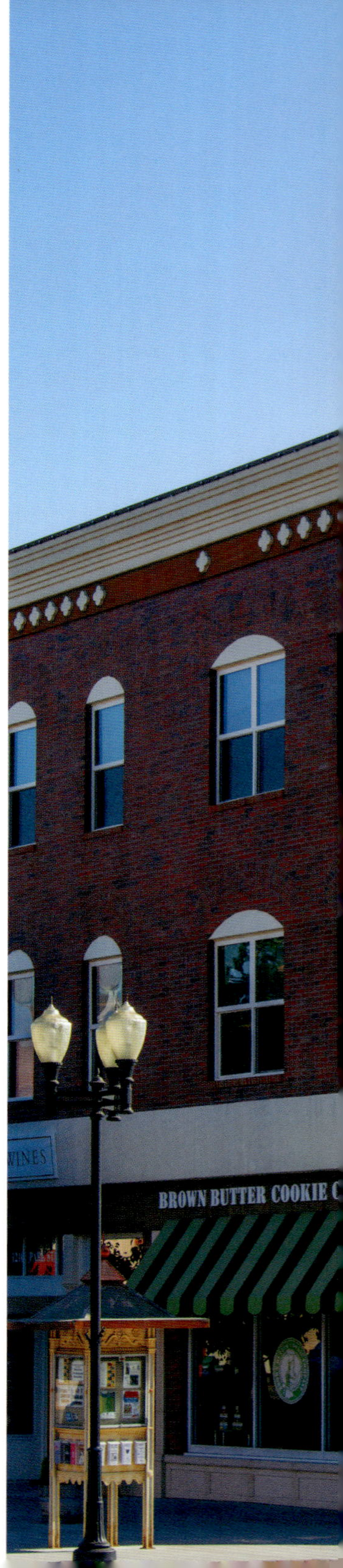

BROWN BUTTER COOKIE

OPPOSITE TOP: We Olive on Park Street features a selection of oils from California olives. OPPOSITE BOTTOM: "Field of Light" fills the hills with thousands of flowerlike lights at Sensorio. LEFT: The Acorn Building, originally built in 1892, is a landmark of downtown.

as well as its world-class tequila bar. Hatch Rotisserie and Bar serves signature roast chicken and sides as well as phenomenal craft cocktails, including a chocolate old-fashioned. Numerous hotels are within walking distance of downtown, including the romantic ivy-covered Hotel Cheval and the Western-inspired boutique Stables Inn, which offers complimentary s'mores kits for its outdoor firepits.

About seven minutes down the road is Tin City, a newer artisanal hub with shops, breweries, wineries, and distilleries set up in repurposed industrial buildings. It's an inspiring and innovative place to spend an afternoon, and the creative energy is palpable. End the day at Sensorio, a multiacre outdoor museum featuring Bruce Munro's otherworldly light installations.

TALK LIKE A LOCAL

"THE 405"

Traffic is no joke in the Golden State. The only way a true native refers to a freeway is with an accompanying article. "Take the 5 to the 10" means to take Interstate 5 to Interstate 10. The 405, a major freeway in Los Angeles and Orange Counties, is the most congested and the busiest interstate in the country; approximately 390,000 cars travel on it every day. Avoid it if you can.

The Solvang Bakery
Wines
Gourmet Foods
440
Homebridge

SOLVANG

CALIFORNIA

The founders of Solvang envisioned a colony where they could live out the American dream while preserving the traditions of Denmark. The name Solvang, which means "sunny field" in Danish, is apt. Tucked away in the Santa Ynez Valley, about 40 minutes north of Santa Barbara, the charming town has been featured in numerous Hallmark Christmas movies and various television series. It's easy to see why. Windmills are nestled among shops and restaurants, and nearly every building is designed in the Danish provincial architecture style, with signature elements like *bindingsverk* (half-timber) walls and faux thatched roofs. Stop in a traditional Danish bakery, like the Solvang Bakery or Mortensen's, to enjoy an almond *kringle* (a flaky, fruit-filled pastry), strudel, or *kransekakestenger* (baked almond marzipan cookies), or pop into the Book Loft to explore antiquarian reads and the Hans Christian Andersen Museum upstairs.

The windmill on Alisal Road is one of six in Solvang, but this is the most photographed of the bunch.

Exceptional food and wine offerings make Solvang a place to return to again and again. Try Peasants Feast, an airy indoor-outdoor restaurant in the heart of town, for lunch or dinner. Light streams in through the restaurant's massive windows, giving it a relaxed greenhouse vibe, and menus are seasonally and locally driven with twists on comfort food dishes, such as a pastrami and smoked salmon sandwich or a Gold Coast grilled cheese made with Gruyère, mozzarella, caramelized onions, and a Parmesan crisp. A short walk away is Coast Range, where

TASTE OF THE REGION

AEBLESKIVER

These puffy Danish pancake balls, dusted with powdered sugar and drizzled with raspberry jam, are a must-have Solvang treat. Bakeries around town offer aebleskiver, so line up wherever is closest to your hotel for a morning pick-me-up or a midday treat. "Aebleskiver" translates to "apple slices" in Danish—the original version was filled with small apple pieces or applesauce, but apples have disappeared from most modern recipes.

The Landsby hotel blends California style with Scandinavian refinement. Guests can enjoy firepits in the courtyard year-round.

a quiet confidence in the atmosphere and welcoming staff greet guests to enjoy out-of-this-world food—the menu changes daily, but think glazed cheese ravioli with lamb leg and tapioca-crusted Thai snapper—and a terrific wine selection.

The boutique hotel Landsby combines traditional Scandinavian aesthetic with contemporary design. It's the ideal place to stay, complete with firepits and lounge chairs in the courtyard. The hotel can also facilitate booking a tour to three local wineries, complete with tastings and car service. Right outside town, Alisal Ranch is a luxury working ranch that welcomes visitors in search of a little adventure with their relaxation. Guest cottages are available for families to enjoy, and the 10,500-acre ranch offers trail rides, a golf course, and numerous outdoor and lake activities. Beautiful views of oak trees with trailing lichen cover the rolling hills. You can start the day with a horseback ride to the historic Adobe Camp, where a classic Western-style breakfast awaits.

The greater Santa Ynez Valley is home to many adorable small towns, all within a short drive of Solvang. Wineries and tasting rooms dot the landscape. Pick up a charcuterie board and gourmet sandwiches from the Lucky Hen Larder on the way to Gainey Vineyard, which has reservation-only flights within a barrel-lined tasting room. Afterward, take your picnic outside among the grapevines and trees. The region averages 300 sunny days per year, so visitors are bound to bask in the sunshine.

ESTES PARK

COLORADO

At the base of Rocky Mountain National Park, Estes Park is the ideal launching pad for numerous outdoor adventures. The town itself boasts plenty to do between hikes among the wildflowers at Gem Lake or scenic drives across the Continental Divide on Trail Ridge Road.

Founded in 1859, Estes Park was put on the map by Enos Mills, a naturalist and conservationist who devoted his life to preserving nearly 1,000 square miles of Colorado as Rocky Mountain National Park (called simply "the Park" by locals). In the 1880s, most visitors came to Estes Park in search of better health. These early visitors included entrepreneurs Freelan Oscar Stanley and Francis Edgar Stanley. After the brothers fell in love with the mountain climate and noticed a dramatic improvement in their health, they opened the Stanley Hotel. The beautiful white Colonial Revival building is still one of the best places to stay in town, and offers many dining options and seasonal events. Most notably, the hotel served as partial inspiration for the Overlook Hotel in Stephen King's *The Shining*. Relive parts of the novel on the Spirited Night Tour, a spine-tingling experience that highlights the history of the hotel and its paranormal activities.

It's not a visit to Estes Park without a trip into Rocky Mountain National Park. Come any time of year. You can take multiday backpacking trips in the summer, hike in the fall (ideal for leaf-peeping

The hike to and from Rocky Mountain National Park's Dream Lake is just 2.2 miles round-trip, and the scenic rewards are vast.

ADVENTURE ALONG THE WAY

LONGS PEAK SCOTTISH-IRISH HERITAGE FESTIVAL

Each September, clans parade and compete in Estes Park's Longs Peak Scottish-Irish Heritage Festival. This highly anticipated event is the town's most attended festival. Celtic music, Irish dancing, jousting, piping competitions, and Highland games bring crowds in the thousands to the mountains of Colorado. Dress in colorful tartans to immerse yourself in the Scots-Irish spirit throughout the week.

With the Big Thompson River in the foreground and the Rockies in the background, it's pretty much impossible to take a bad photograph in Estes Park.

and hearing the bugling of elk), snowshoe in the winter, and fish in the spring. This is one of the most popular national parks in the United States, so it's essential that visitors abide by leave-no-trace principles, as well as the Rocky Pledge: "to preserve unimpaired for this and future generations the beauty, history, and wilderness therein." Reserve a timed-entry permit, especially during peak months (May through September).

In Estes Park proper, stroll down Elkhorn Avenue and stop in its many boutiques. The Taffy Shop is an Estes Park staple. It makes saltwater taffy using the same original recipe as on opening day in 1935; a taffy puller showcases how the special treat is created in a display window. A little outside town is Coffee on the Rocks, a mostly outdoor café next to a charming duck pond. Also outside of town is Cinnamon's Bakery, famous for its cinnamon rolls—grab one with a coffee before heading to Lake Estes to walk the four-mile waterfront loop. From the lake you'll have unobstructed sight lines to Longs Peak. The loop is also one of the few dog-friendly trails in town; pets are not allowed inside the national park. After your hike, check out Avant Garde Aleworks for its firepits, food trucks, and sip-worthy craft beer.

OURAY

COLORADO

Imogene Pass sits at 13,000 feet in the San Juan Mountains, separating the skiing mecca of Telluride from the hidden gem of Ouray. Like many mountain towns in the late 1800s, Ouray was first established by gold prospectors hoping to strike it rich. At the height of the mining era, Ouray had more than 30 active mines. Today, its historic district encompasses nearly the entire town, with a majority of the buildings dating between 1886 and 1915. The Western Hotel and Spa, built in 1891, is among the oldest hotels in Colorado, and one of the few remaining frontier-style wood-framed boardinghouses in the West. It is newly restored and reopened as an elegant boutique hotel. Nearby on Main Street, explore the shops and studios where local artists take up residence and specialize in hand-blown glass, pottery, photography, and other mediums. The Ouray County Historical Society offers a walking tour of the town for just a dollar.

Ouray has been called the outdoor recreation capital of Colorado and is known for the three W's: wildlife, wildflowers, and waterfalls. Yankee Boy Basin and Governor's Basin are two premier hiking spots with spectacular blooms of columbines, lupines, Indian paintbrushes, and alpine sunflowers in the spring. Bear Creek Falls and Box Canyon Falls are just two of the spectacular cascades nearby. The Historic Ouray Hot Springs Pool, open since 1927, is a great spot to relax and unwind after a full day enjoying world-class outdoor adventures.

TASTE OF THE REGION

ROCKY MOUNTAIN OYSTERS

Rocky Mountain Oysters are, in fact, not oysters at all. No, the landlocked state of Colorado embraces its own unique "oyster" delicacy, which is made of deep-fried bull calf testicles, served sliced, with dipping sauce on the side. These "oysters" have a gamy quality, almost like a mix between chicken, venison, and calamari. Don't assume they're just for street cred; you'll find the dish at dive bars and fine-dining establishments alike.

Take a short drive out of Ouray to Yankee Boy Basin, where waterfalls and wildflowers—including paintbrush, chiming bluebells, and dwarf sunflowers—make a spectacular scene.

Salida is called the Heart of the Rockies for a reason. The picturesque town is nestled along the Arkansas River in the Rocky Mountains, about a three-hour drive from Denver. Salida came to be thanks to the gold rush. To meet the demand of the burgeoning populations out West, railroads began to connect the vast American countryside; when the Denver and Rio Grande Railroads reached Salida, this small town was officially born.

A mix of industries made up Salida in 1880: mining, quarrying, smelting, agriculture, and retail trade. Alongside came "related" industries: saloons, gambling, and prostitution—all the makings of a stereotypical Wild West settlement.

The Salida Downtown Historic District is Colorado's largest national historic district, with 111 buildings on the National Register of Historic Places. Sweetie's Sandwich Shop is located in the former parlor house of Laura Evans, Salida's most famous madam, and city hall resides in the Touber Building, formerly the 1885 railroad hospital. The SteamPlant Event Center is in the old steam-powered electric plant, which dates back to 1892. Today, the SteamPlant hosts community yoga classes, a summer concert series, and local theater productions, among hundreds of other events.

The mixing of old and new is evident around every corner. Salida experienced two devastating

Visit the shops, restaurants, and live-music venues near the Salida Riverwalk.

ADVENTURE ALONG THE WAY

MINERAL BELT TRAIL

Leadville, Colorado—an hour north of Salida—is the highest-elevation incorporated city in North America, at 10,152 feet above sea level. The Mineral Belt Trail is an outdoor history museum that surrounds Leadville's historic mining district, looping through aspen trees, wildflower meadows, and remnants of the 1880s mines that contributed to the rise and fall of the area's silver boom. Interpretive signs highlight the movers and shakers of the Colorado silver industry, and mining artifacts showcase the heritage of the region. Consider renting e-bikes to traverse the 11.6-mile loop in one afternoon.

The Arkansas River is full of energy, ideal for kayakers, whitewater rafters, swimmers, and even river surfers.

fires, in 1886 and 1888. The destroyed buildings were rebuilt with locally made bricks, and preserved advertisements and signs from the 1800s still adorn many of these historic buildings.

Salida has a balanced love of the outdoors and the arts. The Creative District, the first such district certified in the state, was transformed from crumbling, derelict buildings into a thriving area by a small community of artists in the 1990s. In addition to the 30 artist-owned or artist-run galleries, the Creative District is made up of restaurants, bars, microbreweries, a distillery, dozens of boutiques, three locally owned bicycle shops, and even a film production studio. Moonlight Pizza and Brewpub is a favorite in this slice of town, as is the Beekeeper's Honey Boutique, which started in 1908 and is the oldest honey company in Colorado. Shop for bee pollen, honeycombs, and crystallized honey pearls.

The summer months in Salida offer a host of outdoor activities. The Arkansas River is one of the most famous draws as the home of America's oldest whitewater festival, First in Boating the Arkansas (FIBArk), a series of premiere athletic boat races that has been held annually since 1949. During non-festival days, you can raft, kayak, or float the river, which runs right off the downtown path Riverwalk. Mountain biking is extremely popular, too, with numerous trails for all skill levels. For hiking, the Alpine Tunnel Trail is a moderate 5.5-mile route that winds along an old railroad past the historic Alpine

OPPOSITE TOP: Stay in an Airstream at Amigo Motor Lodge. OPPOSITE BOTTOM: Enjoy live music at the annual FIBArk festival in Riverside Park. LEFT: The Monarch Crest Trail tops out at 11,960 feet in elevation.

Tunnel train station. The elevation here can take a toll on travelers—Salida is 7,083 feet above sea level—so be sure to take it slow and drink plenty of water. Expert hikers, however, will find 15 fourteeners (mountains that exceed 14,000 feet in elevation) nearby, including Mount Harvard, Chaffee County's highest point and Colorado's third highest peak.

After a day of hiking and exploring, relax at Mount Princeton Hot Springs before bedding down at the coolest motel in town: Amigo Motor Lodge. In 2016, the property, formerly the circa 1950s Aspen Leaf Lodge, was converted into a boutique roadside motel, with private Airstreams included. The aesthetic—vintage southwestern meets modern luxury—is impeccable, and the entire motel is dog friendly, as advertised by the hilarious sign out front: "Dogs welcome. Well-behaved humans, too."

TALK LIKE A LOCAL

"A GAPER"

A gaper is a clueless person on the ski slopes, often standing around and generally getting in the way, usually because they tried a trail that they just weren't ready for yet. Try not be a gaper; stick to runs that match your skill set. The term can also refer to the gap between a ski helmet and goggles—and the resulting tan line.

KŌLOA

HAWAII

Kōloa, the home of Hawaii's first successful sugar mill, sits near Po'ipū Beach on the south shore of Kauai. The arrival of sugar-cane plantations set the course for post-colonial Hawaii and the influx of immigrants that led to the melting pot of Polynesian, Japanese, Portuguese, and Chinese cultures seen in Hawaii today. Kōloa Plantation Days in July is a wonderful time to visit to celebrate the rich history and diverse cultural traditions found on the island.

The 10-mile Kōloa Heritage Trail (Ka Ala Hele Waiwai Ho'oilina o Kōloa) takes hikers on a self-guided tour through Old Town Kōloa's historic buildings and sites, tracing the birth of Hawaii's sugar-plantation era in the 1830s. The Yamamoto Store, built in 1898, and the Okumura Building, constructed in 1905, house boutiques, galleries, and restaurants. The Kahalewai Building, a former World War II military outpost, is now home to Fish Eye Kauai, a must-visit gallery stop while in town.

The gateway to Kōloa is known as the "tree tunnel," a canopy of eucalyptus trees lining a one-mile stretch of Maluhia Road. The trees were first planted a century ago as a gift from pineapple baron Walter McBryde, and they make a fairy-tale entrance to town. There is no shortage of beautiful places to stay along Po'ipū, one of Kauai's best beaches. Wherever you lodge, Little Fish Coffee is a charming breakfast spot to fuel up on fresh acai bowls made with locally sourced ingredients before a day of outdoor activities, such as snorkeling at Lawai Beach or hiking the Maha'ulepu Heritage Trail.

TASTE OF THE REGION

SPAM MUSUBI

A great on-the-go snack found throughout Hawaii, Spam musubi is a slice of grilled Spam on top of a block of rice, wrapped together in nori (dried seaweed). You can enjoy a Spam musubi, a dynamic fusion of Japanese and Hawaiian flavors, with sweet or savory sauces. Some might call it a local take on a protein bar.

The Maha'ulepu Heritage Trail traces a two-mile stretch (four miles round-trip) along the cliffs, in the shadow of Haupu Mountain.

SANDPOINT

IDAHO

There's always something fun to do in Sandpoint, whether it's attending an evening concert in the park as part of the Festival at Sandpoint, or checking out the farmers market at Farmin Park. A great way to fuel your day is with a morning visit to Evans Brothers Coffee Roasters, a funky shop housed in an industrial tin building with vibrant flowerpots, colorful tables, and old coffee sacks tacked on the walls. Don't miss out on a delicious huckleberry muffin with your java. In fact, you should take every opportunity to try the locally grown huckleberries while in Sandpoint. After breakfast, walk the Pend d'Oreille Bay Trail for stunning views of Lake Pend Oreille. Locals use the trail to run or walk and let their dogs cool off in the water. Stop at Foster's Crossing for unique antique finds (the shop is hard to miss, thanks to the massive moose mural on the side of the building). A short drive north from town, find two pick-your-own farm options: Grumpy Chicken Farm for flowers and Shingle Mill Blueberry Farm for blueberries. Shingle Mill is family-owned and -operated and grows several varietals of blueberries.

MickDuff's Brewing Company, housed in the old federal building, is a wonderful representation of the intersection of past and present in Sandpoint. From the time funding for the building was obtained in 1913 to when it finally opened as a post office in 1928, the town underwent tremendous growth. The grand brick structure, built in a blend of Italian Renaissance

Shingle Mill Blueberry Farm is open for berry picking at the height of summer. The farm grows several varieties of blueberries.

TASTE OF THE REGION

HUCKLEBERRY PANCAKES

It's no wonder huckleberries are the official state fruit of Idaho. The tiny, purplish-red wild berries grow in abundance on small evergreen shrubs throughout the state. Huckleberries are a staple at most diners and breakfast spots, and huckleberry pancakes are often the most coveted dish on menus. Peak huckleberry season is from late July to early October, which is also the best time to dig into fluffy sourdough pancakes drenched in huckleberry syrup.

Camp near Lake Pend Oreille for easy access to excellent kayaking opportunities.

Revival and Spanish Colonial Revival styles, was listed on the National Register of Historic Places in 1973. Before its time as a brewery, it also served as a library and an antiques mall. MickDuff's is a gathering place with an outdoor patio equipped for lawn games.

About a 30-minute drive south from downtown Sandpoint is Farragut State Park. Located on the southern tip of Lake Pend Oreille, this 4,000-acre park was formerly a World War II naval training station. Stop by the Museum at the Brig to learn about boot camp and basic training for U.S. Navy recruits in the 1940s. Farragut State Park itself offers a range of outdoor activities, including camping, boating, and birding (keep an eye out for the mountain bluebird, the state bird of Idaho). Hike up the Nature Trail on Schweitzer Mountain to the Nest Restaurant for patio dining and scenic views of Canada, Washington State, Montana, Idaho, and Lake Pend Oreille.

ADVENTURE ALONG THE WAY

INTERNATIONAL SELKIRK LOOP

The International Selkirk Loop encircles the Selkirk Mountains, taking road trippers through Idaho, Washington State, and British Columbia, Canada. The only multinational scenic drive in North America, this 280-mile-long highway passes great small towns along the way and offers plenty of outdoor opportunities. The Idaho portion traverses crystal blue lakes and goes right through Sandpoint.

WALLACE

WALLACE

IDAHO

The small community of Wallace is nestled in the Bitterroot Mountains, about an hour east of Coeur d'Alene. The drive into town feels as though you're traveling back in time, and it's no accident. In 1979, Wallace submitted its entire downtown to the National Register of Historic Places; it has preserved its beautiful architecture even while incorporating modern businesses. Wallace Brewing Company, for example, is in the circa 1890 Coeur d'Alene Hardware building, the Tin Snug record shop and café is in a former funeral home, and the Fainting Goat Restaurant and Bar is housed inside the Finch Building, originally built in 1892. When dining out, pay attention to Wallace's unique restaurant hours: The downtown restaurants alternate closures during the week to ensure that proprietors and staff can enjoy days off. That sense of community perpetuates an earned sense of town pride—even a town ego. In 2004, Wallace formally declared itself the "Center of the Universe," and it holds a rededication ceremony for this title every year.

The best time to visit Wallace is during one of its many festivals, such as the Huckleberry Festival in August. The summer also brings great opportunities for hiking. The Pulaski Tunnel Trail leads trekkers alongside a lovely stream on a fern-lined path. A day of history, meanwhile, might include visiting the bordellos on the north side of Cedar Street. There were four working brothels up until 1988, when the FBI raided the area and shut them down for good. The Oasis Bordello is now a museum that tells the story of Madame Ginger, who, reacting to a tip that FBI agents were sweeping the mountain, fled from the authorities with "her girls." When the Oasis changed hands its new owners discovered that the former bordello had been left almost exactly as it was, down to the cigarettes left in ashtrays, and turned it into a museum. (The museum underwent significant renovations in 2022.) Visit for a look at Wallace's storied past and to learn how the bordellos were a respected fixture of the community.

Explore the Northern Pacific Railroad Depot Museum, which has a replica turn-of-the-20th-century railroad agent's room, where visitors can use a phone from 1908.

RED LODGE

MONTANA

There's a rugged beauty and authentic Western feel to the town of Red Lodge. Beartooth Mountain makes a staggering backdrop, and Rock Creek runs right through downtown along U.S. Route 212, here known as the Beartooth Highway. For visitors, the peaceful atmosphere might inspire a deep, soulful longing to soak in the natural wonders of the scenery.

With Billings only an hour away, Red Lodge has become a great weekend destination. It is not uncommon to walk outside in the morning and see a whitetail deer, a moose, or a black bear shuffling around in a yard. Dramatic sunrises outline the mountain range in vibrant pinks, purples, and oranges. Drive the Beartooth Highway from Red Lodge to the northeastern entrance of Yellowstone National Park to experience some of Montana's most beautiful terrain. The elevation at the top of the pass is nearly 11,000 feet above sea level. Vista Point is a popular place to take in the spectacular views.

This area was home to the Crow people long before the arrival of white settlers. It was a place for the Crow to worship, rest, and hunt during the summer months. In 1887, the Rocky Fork Coal Company opened a mine here, bringing a rush of immigrants and a new leading economic industry. Plenty of legendary events from the early days of the American West took place in burgeoning Red Lodge. Most infamously, the Sundance Kid, an outlaw and member of Butch Cassidy's Wild Bunch,

The stretch of U.S. Route 212 between Red Lodge and Cooke City, Montana, is called the Beartooth Highway. It leads travelers past this iconic view of Beartooth Pass.

TALK LIKE A LOCAL

"MONTANA SHOESHINE"

Almost two million cattle graze across the myriad ranches stretching across Montana. If you're unlucky enough to step in a pile of cow manure, you've got yourself a Montana shoeshine. Don't moan about it, or you'll be told to "cowboy up" or "cowgirl up" by a local Montanan. Translation: Stop whining, scrape off your shoe, and move on with your day.

Montana Candy Emporium on Broadway Avenue sells dozens of candy varieties and is open seven days a week.

attempted to rob a Red Lodge bank in 1897. The local sheriff chased the Sundance Kid for 80 miles before capturing him and returning him to jail in Deadwood, South Dakota—where the outlaw promptly escaped again.

Ranching and recreation eventually replaced coal as the main commercial enterprises. Today, Red Lodge feels like a tale of two small towns, with the working agricultural sect contributing to the Western atmosphere, and the skiers at Red Lodge Mountain putting it on the map as a resort destination. Red Lodge doesn't feel touristy, though; you can walk into a cowboy bar after a day on the trails and share a cold one with the local ranchers—in the summertime, Snow Creek Saloon hosts live music in a divey atmosphere. Those seeking a quieter scene should head to Red Lodge Ales, a brewery that taps into the long history of Montana beermaking by creating brews with fresh glacial water and state-grown barley. The patio is idyllic on a summer afternoon, and the fireplace inside is a great place to cozy up in the winter months. In summer, stop by Babcock and Miles to curate a to-go charcuterie board for a picnic, ride bikes around town, or test your limits on the Face of the Mountain, a switchback-heavy trail along the original road to Beartooth Pass. End the day with margaritas at Bogart's, which calls itself a "best-Mex" restaurant and is a Red Lodge institution.

CHEW MAIL POUCH SMOKE
TREAT YOURSELF TO THE BEST
Pepsi-Cola 5¢
Mobiloils
PEPSI
Honeydew Taffy

WHITEFISH

MONTANA

Whitefish is pure magic. Glacier National Park sits to the east, Whitefish Lake sits to the west, and a downtown historic railway district sits somewhere in the middle. The warmer months are ideal for hitting the hiking trails and visiting City Beach; the colder months are perfect for skiing and snowshoeing. In fact, there's no bad time to visit this gem. The sheer beauty of Montana is hard to put into words, but the town of Whitefish, and the surrounding area, does a wonderful job of showcasing the best of it.

Whitefish has beckoned people since long before the United States was settled. The Kootenai lived in this region for more than 14,000 years, sharing hunting and gathering grounds with the Salish people. In the mid-1850s, a group of beaver trappers working the waters surrounding the Flathead Valley came upon a group of Kootenai pulling a native fish out of a long and narrow lake. The lake was thus christened Whitefish and, after the railroad arrived in 1904, so was the small townsite nearby. Today, Whitefish is home to about 8,500 permanent residents and is an outdoor enthusiast's paradise, with fantastic gastronomic options and beautiful places to stay.

Hidden Moose Lodge, about a five-minute drive from downtown, is emblematic of the Whitefish experience. Find tasteful fish and moose decor, ski

Whitefish Mountain Resort is known as a family-friendly ski destination. Intermediate skiers can dare the Hell Fire run, a 2.5-mile trail through Hellroaring Basin.

TASTE OF THE REGION

MONTANA MEATLOAF

Bison and elk roam the rugged Montana countryside and can be found on many restaurant menus throughout the West. Montana meatloaf is a mixture of beef, bison, and elk. The tender meatloaf is sometimes wrapped in bacon, and often served with a huckleberry glaze. Although you'll find the dish in restaurants throughout Glacier County, the best in show is the elk meatloaf at Whitefish's Tupelo Grille.

Auroras are sometimes visible in Glacier National Park. Clear skies over Lake McDonald invite vast views.

lifts repurposed as benches, and red Adirondack chairs overlooking Whitefish Lake. The lodge hosts a complimentary happy hour with local wine and beer. At breakfast, be sure to ask the owner for hiking recommendations. The Swift Creek Trail is a particularly good one; it's an easy two-mile loop with lush trees and greenery, perfect for families or for those wanting just a small taste of the outdoors. For those wanting a more extensive wilderness experience, the entrance to Glacier National Park is only an hour away. In total, hikers and backpackers have 734 miles of trails to choose from in Glacier National Park, but for those who want to enjoy the view without the walk, the historic Going-to-the-Sun Road is a sweeping drive (just be sure to obtain a vehicle reservation during the peak summer season). Time your park visit to watch a sunrise or sunset over prominent snowcapped peaks. Lucky visitors might even glimpse the northern lights over Lake McDonald. For another outdoor excursion, drive 30 minutes south of Whitefish to Flathead Lake, the largest natural freshwater lake west of the Mississippi.

Whitefish Mountain Resort on Big Mountain is a must-visit for snow sports. As a mural in town aptly states: "Be brave. Take the hill." Beginners can enjoy a scenic mountain tour on the green-level Home Again run, and intermediate skiers can view the whole of the Flathead Valley on Inspiration run; for experts, there's the fresh powder of Hellroaring

OPPOSITE TOP: The Craggy Range in downtown Whitefish regularly features live music. **OPPOSITE BOTTOM:** Adrenaline junkies will find plenty of zip lines in Whitefish; Whitefish Mountain Resort has six. **LEFT:** For classic atmosphere, stay at Hidden Moose Lodge.

Basin. After a full day on the slopes, head into town to explore exceptional boutiques along Central Avenue, like Cabin Creek Antiques and Mum's Flowers. Blackstar is the place to grab a beer, with views of Depot Park, Whitefish Lake, and Big Mountain from the roof-deck.

For dining before or after a day on the mountain, locals say you can't beat breakfast at the Buffalo Café or, for a ski-lodge vibe, nachos at the Hellroaring Saloon. Stop by Tupelo Grille in the evening for live music, a wonderful wine list, and delicious local cuisine—particularly in the summer when you can sit outside. When it's hot outside, visit Clydesdale Creamery for obscenely large milkshakes.

ADVENTURE ALONG THE WAY

LAKE KOOCANUSA SCENIC BYWAY

Beginning in Eureka, Montana, about an hour northwest of Whitefish and close to the Canadian border, is the 67-mile Lake Koocanusa Scenic Byway. The corridor runs along the Kootenai River and Lake Koocanusa and cuts through a narrow fjordlike gorge between the Purcell and Salish Mountains. The clear blue water is jaw-dropping, as are the vistas that unfold around every bend. Bighorn sheep graze the mountainsides, and recreational activities like boating, fishing, and camping are available at stops along the way.

ELY

NEVADA

Beginning as a mining and smelting camp in 1878, for a time Ely was just a stop along the Pony Express. But about 10 years after the town's founding, Nevada's state legislature designated Ely as White Pine County's seat of government, resulting in booming business development. Copper, gold, and silver ore were the main commodities, and today you can take in that history at Ward Charcoal Ovens State Historic Park, a scenic forested retreat. The park features six 30-foot-tall beehive-shaped charcoal ovens from the late 1870s. The ovens were once used to process silver ore, but they also sheltered travelers and stagecoach bandits (when not in use, of course). Visitors can step inside while camping, hiking, and fishing in the park. For another outdoor paradise, check out Cave Lake State Park, which offers fishing and boating in the summer and ice fishing and snowmobiling in the winter.

Ward Charcoal Ovens State Historic Park contains pieces of mining history, namely six beehive ovens used in the 19th century to process silver ore.

A rich archaeological history surrounds Ely. White River Narrows Archaeological District is on the National Register of Historic Places and features Indigenous rock art dating back some 4,000 years. Baker Archaeological Site sits outside Great Basin National Park and has evidence of structures inhabited by the Fremont dating to around A.D. 1200.

After exploring the rugged eastern Nevada landscape, stop in the Ely Renaissance Village to experience the homelife of the miners, railroad workers, sheepherders, and ranchers who built the town.

ADVENTURE ALONG THE WAY

PARK TO PARK IN THE DARK

Dubbed the "Starry-est Route in America," Nevada's first astro-tourism trail connects two International Dark Sky Parks, Death Valley National Park and Great Basin National Park. The 300-mile drive offers some of the best stargazing in the United States, including possible views of galaxies, star clusters, nebulae, and enough stars to satisfy any astronomy, astrology, and cosmology enthusiast. Be sure to fuel your car properly for the trip—cell service and gas stations are rare as you cross the state.

HOOD RIVER

OREGON

The scenic one-hour drive from Portland to Hood River winds along the Columbia River, giving just a taste of the natural beauty that is to come. One local resident shared their favorite part of living in Hood River as being able to see "every shade of green you can imagine." Whether you're seeking a family-friendly getaway, an outdoorsy guys' or girls' trip, or a romantic escape, Hood River has something for everyone.

Hood River is often referred to as Portland's backyard, and with such a mixture of activities, it's easy to see why. Take a morning to drive the delightful Hood River Fruit Loop, a 35-mile scenic route stretching from downtown to the hills of the Columbia Gorge. The Hood River Valley's rich agricultural heritage began with the planting of fruit trees in 1855. Today, the region boasts 14,500 acres of cherry, pear, and apple trees. Along the way are wineries, breweries, and pick-your-own farms worthy of a stop. Hood River Lavender Farms is a particular slice of heaven. For a few bucks, you get to pick all the lavender a zip-top bag can hold, while bees and butterflies flit about and a view of Mount Adams dominates the background. Check out the Lavender Daze Festival in July for live music, food, art, and family activities. Move on to Mt. View Orchards and the Grateful Vineyard for a good meal, which entails a three-course pizza spread and a sampling of ales, lagers, ciders, and wines. Whether you sit inside the tasting room with

The Hood River Valley is renowned for its pears. Keep an eye out for pear desserts like kuchen and dumplings at local restaurants.

TASTE OF THE REGION

COFFEE

Starbucks, which first opened in Seattle in 1971, launched a demand for high-quality locally roasted beans. Soon after, artisanal roasters began to emerge across the Pacific Northwest. Some coffee experts say Portland is the true coffee capital of the world (sorry, Seattle!), and it was Stumptown Coffee Roasters, which opened in the city in 1999, that put it on top.

Hood River's nightlife continues the adventure from a day of outdoor activities.

floor-to-ceiling windows offering views of Mount Hood or outside in the sunshine, there isn't a bad spot to enjoy and sip. Wy'East Vineyards gives oenophiles an opportunity to relax on rocking chairs while enjoying sweeping vistas of alpaca pastures, grapevines, and wildflowers. Started as a fruit stand in the 1940s, this family-owned and -operated vineyard is a wonderful place to slow down and enjoy your surroundings.

Downtown Hood River is packed with boutiques, bookshops, and galleries, and is home to Mike's Ice Cream, a beloved after-dinner spot where it seems the whole town gathers. The community-minded, family-owned shop has been in its teal-colored storefront since 1986. Their scoops include flavors like raspberry truffle and peppermint. The Hood River Hotel is a great place to call home for your stay. Built in 1911, the hotel has updated historic rooms with views of the Columbia River Gorge. Broder Øst, a wonderful breakfast spot to fill up on Swedish-style breakfast, or *frukost,* is attached to the lobby. Order the *lefse* breakfast (a Norwegian-style potato crepe stuffed with chèvre and topped with baked eggs), aebleskiver (Danish pancake balls served with lingonberry jam and house lemon curd), and cardamom coffee.

The Waterfront is a newly transformed riverfront path with kiteboarding and windsurfing launches, as well as a family park. Stop in at Ferment Brewing Company, where you'll find an indoor-outdoor

OPPOSITE TOP: Go windsurfing at the Spring Creek Hatchery near the Columbia River Gorge. OPPOSITE BOTTOM: Broder Øst serves Danish pancakes with lingonberry jam. LEFT: Hood River Lavender Farms offers a more relaxed outdoor experience.

tasting room built with mixed materials such as concrete, metal, and wood planks. It's an inviting and just plain cool environment. Sit on the patio and enjoy delicious smoked salmon dip, Nilgiri black tea kombucha, and excellent craft beer.

During the warmer months, the span of the Columbia River near Hood River is called the "windsurfing capital of the world." Spot the colorful sails during Hood Jam, a premier kiteboarding competition held in July for riders from all over the globe. For an adventure of another kind, hop on a two-person railbike and pedal along the Hood River, past a waterfall and lush pine trees, on the Mount Hood Railroad. Trains also use these tracks, including seasonal options that explore the area's orchards and vineyards in the summer and fall and a Polar Express train around the holidays.

TALK LIKE A LOCAL

"THE MOUNTAIN IS OUT"

Days in the Pacific Northwest are often cloudy and drizzly. However, on sunny days with clear blue skies, Oregonians will remark that "the mountain is out," meaning that you can see Mount Hood near Portland. Locals love to take advantage of the sun, and when the mountain is out, it means a good day lies ahead.

JACKSONVILLE

OREGON

In the heart of southern Oregon's Rogue Valley sits the town of Jacksonville, or J'Ville as the locals call it. Beginning as a gold rush town in the 1850s, it developed into a hub of commerce and eventually became the county seat of government. In 1884, the railroad bypassed Jacksonville in favor of Medford, and many residents and businesses, as well as the county government, moved away, leaving original buildings intact as a time capsule downtown. J'Ville was sleepy for several decades, but in the 1950s an influx of artists and vintners began to reinvigorate the town. Today, it's known as the gateway to the Applegate Valley Wine Trail.

Jacksonville is infused with historic charm and artistic flair. The annual summerlong Britt Music and Arts Festival is a huge draw. Downtown is packed with independently owned shops and restaurants, like Bella Union, where you can enjoy pizza and live music on a tree-canopy-shaded patio, and the Restaurant at Jacksonville Inn, which serves locally sourced meals.

Opportunities abound to take in nature around town. The Jacksonville Rail Trail takes hikers along a former railroad bed dating to 1916. The East Applegate Ridge Trail winds through meadows of wildflowers. Keep an eye out for Gentner's fritillaries, a rare native flower—the surrounding woodlands host one of the largest concentrations of it in the world. Enjoy the beauty of the valley at one of the unique wineries nearby. Valley View Winery encourages visitors to bring a picnic to enjoy on the lawn.

The Britt Music and Arts Festival brings the Jacksonville community together every summer. Take a blanket with you for lawn seating at Britt Pavilion.

ADVENTURE ALONG THE WAY

OREGON COAST TRAIL

The beauty of the Oregon coastline unfolds through every twist and turn of the Oregon Coast Trail, or OCT. Stretching 362 miles, the OCT passes 28 beach towns and countless wooded forests, vistas overlooking headlands, and plunging cliffs. The trail is more commonly broken into sections and used for day hikes rather than thru-hikes.

SISTERS

OREGON

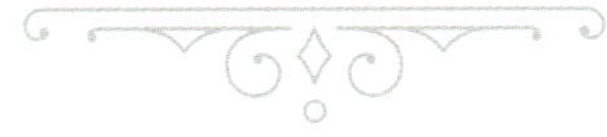

Named for the three towering volcanic peaks to the west of town—Faith, Hope, and Charity, more commonly known as the Three Sisters—artsy Sisters, Oregon, packs a punch of personality. The buildings in this one-roundabout town are clad in 1880 Western facades, an old-time movie house gives a taste of nostalgia with craft beer on the side, and the culinary scene ranges from upscale at the Open Door wine bar to casual at High Camp Taphouse.

Sisters is a great base for outdoor enthusiasts wishing to hike the Cascade peaks, cycle the 37-mile Sisters to Smith Rock Scenic Bikeway, or plunge into the crystal blue waters at Clear Lake. The Sisters Stampede mountain bike race in May is the biggest such competition in the state, with participants traversing the Peterson Ridge Trails. Two annual events in the summer kick off peak season and showcase the diverse array of Sisters attractions: The first is the Sisters Outdoor Quilt Show, the largest outdoor quilt show in the world, representing global fiber artists with more than 1,300 quilts. The second is the Sisters Rodeo, aka the Biggest Little Show in the World. The rodeo attracts world champions who compete for some of the highest purses offered in the nation. For year-round entertainment, visit the Belfry off Main Street, a church built in 1914 turned retro concert venue. The Sisters Art Stroll happens every fourth Friday, and the Sisters Farmers Market hosts live music every Sunday, connecting Oregon farmers with the community. Day or night, Sisters has something to offer.

The Sisters Outdoor Quilt Show takes place each summer. The weeklong festival literally blankets the town in unique handcrafted decor.

ADVENTURE ALONG THE WAY

WILLAMETTE NATIONAL FOREST

When most people hear "Willamette," they think of the wines of the Willamette Valley, but Oregon's Willamette National Forest, just an hour outside of Sisters, is another treasure worth exploring. Its 1.6 million acres are home to seven major peaks and plenty of hiking and biking trails, including numerous waterfall trails.

GARDEN CiTY

UTAH

Summertime in Garden City means days on Bear Lake, enjoying the brilliant turquoise water and munching on handfuls of world-famous Bear Lake raspberries. Sometimes referred to as the Caribbean of the Rockies, Bear Lake offers a serene atmosphere, lively outdoor energy, and sublime water.

The late summer raspberry harvest yields opportunities to grab a raspberry shake or visit a roadside stand for fresh-picked fruit. The three-day Bear Lake Raspberry Days Festival, held in August at the end of harvest season, is a great way to enjoy all that Garden City has to offer. On Bear Lake itself, visitors can enjoy beaches, boating, swimming, and even scuba diving. Stay at Conestoga Ranch to take full advantage of the lake's activities. Glamping sites have luxurious tents and wagons overlooking the water. And there's no better way to end the day than sitting by the campfire watching the sunset.

Freshwater Bear Lake is famously clear, making it ideal for snorkeling or paddling. For a break from the water, search the surrounding valley for wild raspberries.

If water activities aren't your thing, Uinta-Wasatch-Cache National Forest borders the town and has 1,700 miles of hiking, biking, and horseback riding trails to tackle. On the south end of Bear Lake Boulevard, the Pickleville Playhouse is known for quirky melodramas and Broadway musicals. Catching a show in the historic log theater is a fun way to spend your evening. The laid-back environment and incredible scenery of Garden City are why families return annually for a weekend retreat.

ADVENTURE ALONG THE WAY

SKI UTAH

While you may visit Garden City for summer activities, come winter, it's just a two-hour drive to Ogden and Eden, destinations known for their ski resorts, including Snowbasin, Powder Mountain, and Nordic Valley. (Ogden is also home to George S. Eccles Dinosaur Park known for its life-size replicas.) Park City, home to the Park City Mountain and Deer Valley Resorts, is also about two hours from Garden City.

MOAB

UTAH

On the road into Moab, rust-red sandstone arches and spires dot the surrounding desert landscape, and staggering cliffs reach high on both sides. The landscapes here are truly jaw-dropping, and that's to say nothing of the several national and state parks close by.

Moab is often called the biggest adult-adventure playground in the United States. The town sits along the Colorado River, and the bold will jump at the numerous rafting opportunities available, which range from family-friendly to wilder whitewater rapids. If visiting Moab during the hot summer months, a rafting trip through the epic canyons is a great way to keep cool.

Despite the heat, spring and summer are generally considered the best times of year to make Moab a base for visiting nearby parks. Just a 10-minute drive away, Arches National Park has the world's largest concentration of natural sandstone arches. Consider arriving in the early hours and hiking to Delicate Arch to catch the sunrise. There's nothing quite like watching the red sandstone come alive with the morning sun. The park caters to all levels of hiking enthusiasts, and trails crisscross its vast 76,519 acres. Canyonlands National Park, about 30 minutes away, is Utah's largest national park at 337,598 acres. It's divided into distinct districts carved by the Colorado and Green Rivers: Island in the Sky, the Maze, and the Needles. Each offers a

The hike to Delicate Arch is as beautiful as the destination. Keep your footing if you venture out for a photo op beneath the arch.

TASTE OF THE REGION

FRY SAUCE

Fry sauce is a Utah staple made from a proprietary mix of mayonnaise, ketchup, and secret spices. Sweet and tangy, this ultimate dipping condiment has relatives across the globe: *salsa golf* in Argentina, *kokteilsósa* in Iceland, and Marie Rose sauce in the United Kingdom. Utahns worth their salt, however, will die on the hill that fry sauce originated in the Beehive State in the late 1940s, when Don Carlos Edwards, founder of the fast-food chain Arctic Circle, first concocted the now world-famous sauce.

Sorrel River Ranch places lodgers right on the Colorado River. There are few more peaceful places to unwind after a day of hiking.

plethora of outdoor adventures and plenty to see, including buttes, arches, spires, and high desert. Dead Horse Point State Park, 30 minutes outside Moab, has the Intrepid Trail System, which is built for mountain bikers. Its 17 miles are for nonmotorized use only and wind through juniper and pinyon trees and over slick rock. Bikers of all levels can come here to bike the family-friendly beginner trails or the more extreme expert-only terrain. Cyclists should also try the Whole Enchilada biking trail, which starts in Moab and loops for 35 miles around town and the surrounding desert.

Stay immersed in nature at Sorrel River Ranch, a serene luxury resort along the Colorado River near Canyonlands. Relax on a porch swing with views of red-rock mesas, pluck fresh veggies from Sorrel Garden, and book curated experiences such as a hot-air balloon ride or canyoneering in the parks. Field Station Moab is a laid-back, adventure-based hotel a bit closer to town. There's a gear shop and on-site rentals to help outfit your daily excursions. A hot tub and firepit invite guests to mingle and swap stories.

For a break from the outdoors, explore Moab proper's local charms. Moonflower Community Cooperative is a great spot to pick up goodies for a picnic. Doughbird serves mouthwatering cronuts and chicken and waffles (arrive early, before they sell out). Moab Food Truck Park is a fun gathering spot with classic street fare. The park is open from

MOAB
MADE
OPEN

OPPOSITE TOP: The Intrepid Trail System at Dead Horse Point State Park has family-friendly mountain bike trails. OPPOSITE BOTTOM: Downtown Moab offers a number of quirky art boutiques. LEFT: Rafting on the Colorado River nestles you amid towering red plateaus.

11 a.m. to 9 p.m. and features a rotating cast of mobile food spots, including Street Dogs (gourmet hot dogs), Big Don's Pizza and Pasta, and Miss Gelato for something sweet. Woody's Tavern is a great place to grab a beer and enjoy live music.

Moab Valley is part of the Ute ancestral homeland. Indigenous peoples, including the Ute, Navajo, Paiute, and Hopi, have inhabited the region for millennia. Cliff dwellings and petroglyphs offer a glimpse into the history of the ancestral Puebloan and Fremont people, who flourished here in farming communities dating back 10,000 years. Moab carefully preserves the spiritual and energetic connection to the past, intent on keeping it a beautiful place for generations to come.

ADVENTURE ALONG THE WAY

COYOTE BUTTES NORTH

Only 64 people per day are given permits to Coyote Buttes North (aka the Wave), located on the Arizona-Utah border near Kanab in the Paria Canyon-Vermilion Cliffs Wilderness, about five hours from Moab. Permits are hard-won via a lottery system, but the views in this terrain are spectacular and worth the effort. Bright red and orange sandstone dunes have calcified in wavy, swirling vertical and horizontal patterns that seem otherworldly. A six-mile unmarked hike brings you to the unique terrain—it's not recommended during the heat of summer.

LA CONNER

WASHINGTON

La Conner is a self-proclaimed "tiny town with big charm." Surrounded by tulip fields and farmland to the west and the evergreen-lined Swinomish Channel to the east, La Conner is just an hour north of Seattle and within a stone's throw of the Canadian border. Come here for a packed day trip or a relaxed weekend retreat. Driving into town, you'll pass farm stands selling zucchini, pumpkins, tulip bulbs, and berries. Flower vendors, such as La Conner Rotary Club's tulip stand, dot the roads, and colorful hydrangeas bloom in overgrown bushes in the spring and summer. Crab boats with well-worn fishing nets float along the channel, framing the Rainbow Bridge. The air feels salty and smells of the sea and evergreens.

In April, La Conner's Skagit Valley Tulip Festival is *the* destination event for the Pacific Northwest. More than 50 tulip varieties stretch throughout the valley, bringing La Conner a huge splash of color and an atmosphere of joyful romance. La Conner Channel Lodge's surrounding wildflowers will keep you immersed in the blooming beauty; it sits along the water and beckons visitors with its cedar-shake building, wooden balconies, and lush flora. Walk out the front door of the lodge and directly into town to explore the boutiques and restaurants along First Avenue. Stop at Handmade La Conner for artisanal soaps made on-site and

Tulip Town in nearby Mount Vernon is one of many farms that participate in the Skagit Valley Tulip Festival.

ADVENTURE ALONG THE WAY

SNOQUALMIE FALLS

The awe-inspiring falls, one of the most scenic attractions in Washington State, are about an hour and a half south of La Conner. Spruce, Douglas fir, and hemlock trees grow alongside the waterway, and you're more likely than not to see a rainbow glistening in the cascade's spray. A short hike on a winding, forested pathway will take you to the lower observation deck. The roar of the famous 270-foot Snoqualmie Falls can quite literally shake the deck you're standing on. The observation area is open from dawn until dusk, and it's worth sticking around to see lights illuminating the falls as the sun begins to set.

La Conner Channel Lodge is the town's only waterfront hotel. It includes relaxing gardens on the property and a river-rock fireplace in the lobby.

Wood Merchant for hand-carved home decor. La Conner Brewing Company is a lively lunch spot, with a bright and hoppy blood orange IPA and local artists' works on the walls. Its food menu includes braised pork enchiladas, a brie burger with roasted garlic aioli, and eight varieties of wood-fired pizza. Have dinner along the water at Nell Thorn Waterfront Bistro and Bar, where your views are accompanied by delicious farm-to-table dishes including morel pasta (a house-made tagliatelle with sautéed wild morels) and polpetta pomodoro made with American Wagyu. For something sweet, head to La Conner Ice Cream Tower for its waterfront views and rotating menu of ice cream flavors. Then stroll along the boardwalk to Gilkey Square, where you can take in live music on Sunday afternoons.

Artists settled here in the 1940s and established the area as a haven for art lovers and creatives alike. Two museums in town are must-see stops. The first is the Pacific Northwest Quilt and Fiber Arts Museum, housed in the Gaches Mansion, a 22-room home built in 1891. Friendly docents are eager to share the works of quilters and artists from around the world, and the mansion itself is a pristine Victorian, complete with the trademark octagonal tower on one side and a widow's walk on the rooftop. On the more modern side of things, the Museum of Northwest Art is in a gorgeous modernist building in the heart of downtown.

OPPOSITE TOP: Take a boat tour under the Rainbow Bridge, which connects La Conner to the Swinomish Indian Reservation. **OPPOSITE BOTTOM:** Visit the Museum of Northwest Art for local exhibits. **LEFT:** Nell Thorn Waterfront Bistro and Bar features Pacific Northwest cuisine.

A drive over the Rainbow Bridge takes visitors across the Swinomish Channel to Fidalgo Island. The island is home to the Swinomish Indian Reservation and the Kukutali Preserve, the first tribal state park in the history of the United States to be co-owned and managed by a state government and a federally recognized Native American tribe. For more Indigenous history, take an easy two-mile hike to Kiket Island, about 14 minutes from La Conner through an ancestral foodway of the Swinomish people. Be sure to visit at low tide, as the walkways between Similk Bay and Kiket Bay can become covered by water. For another outdoor excursion, kayak toward Skagit Bay to visit the abandoned, moss-covered Fort Whitman on Goat Island. Be sure to obtain a Discover Pass—a combined ticket for access to parks and recreation areas—before a visit.

TASTE OF THE REGION

RAINIER CHERRIES

Named after Mount Rainier, the highest peak in Washington State, and developed at Washington State University in 1952 by Harold Fogle, deliciously sweet Rainier cherries have a golden-yellow hue with a slight red flush. Rainier cherry season is short—from mid-June to late July. The cherries are best enjoyed freshly picked or raw in a salad—they aren't the best for baking.

PORT TOWNSEND

WASHINGTON

Port Townsend, about two hours from Seattle, guards Puget Sound on the northeast corner of the Olympic Peninsula. This town was once called the City of Dreams when early settlers speculated that it would become the largest harbor on the Pacific coast. Although those hopes were never quite realized, this coastal town has become a weekend destination, with well-preserved Victorian-era architecture and abundant natural beauty.

Located on the ancestral land of the S'Klallam people, Port Townsend was founded in 1851 in anticipation of its becoming the northern terminus of the Union Pacific transcontinental railroad line. The railroad promise caused a boom of building in the downtown district, but when funds ran out before the completion of the line, many of those buildings were abandoned. What was left behind inadvertently became the only largely intact Victorian seaport on the West Coast.

The Port Townsend Wooden Boat Festival brings traditional watercraft to the marina every September.

All along Water Street are unique boutiques, restaurants, and cafés. Stop in World's End for steampunk- and pirate-inspired goods; grab gourmet treats from Getables; hunt for funky antiques at Magpie Alley; or rent a bike for the day from the Broken Spoke. The Palace Hotel, in a beautifully renovated 1889 building, is convenient to downtown. This landmark building once operated as a brothel under the nickname the Palace of Sweets. Today, its rooms are named for the women who once worked there. Nearby is the Bishop Block Bottle Shop, in the historic boutique Bishop Hotel. It's an idyllic café and wine bar set in a garden courtyard,

TALK LIKE A LOCAL

"SEATTLE TUXEDO"

You've officially become a Washingtonian when your typical outfit is jeans and a flannel shirt or fleece (preferably black and from REI or the North Face). That's known as a Seattle tuxedo, acceptable to wear any time of year to any kind of establishment, from the most casual diner to the most elegant restaurant.

The three-story Palace Hotel on Water Street in historic downtown dates to 1889.

complete with firepits and live music in the evenings. Chetzemoka City Park, dedicated to S'Klallam chief Chetzemoka in 1904, offers trails to the beach, views of the Cascade Mountains, and a replica of the town's original Victorian bandstand, where you can still picnic or watch events. The Port Townsend Wooden Boat Festival in September immerses visitors in the maritime culture of the Pacific Northwest.

When in Port Townsend, getting on the water is a must. The area is one of the best places for whale- and dolphin-watching in the United States (keep an eye out for orcas, too), so join a guided tour. Sailing and boating activities abound as well. The Northwest Maritime Center is a great hub for sailing classes and water tours aboard the *Admiral Jack*. Kayak or paddleboard around the waters of Fort Worden, Admiralty Inlet, and Port Townsend Bay to soak in the spectacular scenery on your own.

TASTE OF THE REGION

SALMON CANDY

Salmon candy is a Pacific Northwest delicacy with Native American roots. To make this sweet-savory treat, pieces of fresh-caught sockeye or Chinook salmon are hung in a smokehouse, covered with a molasses- or brown sugar-based syrup, and hot smoked until almost completely dry. The sweet, smoky, and salty candy is considered a healthy snack that you can eat as is or enjoy atop a bagel or salad.

1004
PALACE HOTEL
LOBBY
ENTERTAINMENT

·BUFFALO BILL·
MDCCCXLVI - MCMXVII ·

CODY

WYOMING

Wyoming's gateway to Yellowstone National Park, Cody is filled with Wild West history and opportunities for scenic outdoor excursions. Three mountain ranges surround the town: the Bighorn Mountains to the east, the Owl Creek Mountains to the south, and the Absaroka Range to the west. Indigenous peoples, including the Plains and Shoshone, originally inhabited this land. Due to treaties between white settlers and these tribes, the Bighorn Basin remained one of the last frontiers settled in the lower 48. Restrictions on settlement remained in place until the late 1800s; William F. "Buffalo Bill" Cody founded Cody in 1896. Today, the town's Buffalo Bill Center of the West documents the saga of the Wild West with five museums on its campus. The Draper Natural History Museum is a kid-friendly exploration of the ecosystems, wildlife, and plants in the area. Meanwhile, more than 300 paintings and sculptures of Western American art are on display in the Whitney Western Art Museum, the Buffalo Bill Museum celebrates the greatest cowboys and cowgirls of the Wild West, and the Cody Firearms Museum houses the most comprehensive collection of American firearms in the world. Finally, the lives, cultures, and traditions of the Plains Indian communities are honored in the Plains Indian Museum.

All summer long, Cody hosts the Cody Nite Rodeo and the Cody Stampede to pay homage to the legend of Buffalo Bill and his Wild West show. Dating back to in 1919, these nightly events are the longest-running professional rodeos in the

A sculpture of Buffalo Bill Cody himself welcomes you to the Buffalo Bill Center of the West, where a bevy of museums feature exhibits on Native American history, natural history, and Western art.

ADVENTURE ALONG THE WAY

JACKALOPE CITY

The official mythical creature in the state of Wyoming (yes, it's a thing) is the jackalope, a jackrabbit with antelope horns. An oversize jackalope, once the world's largest, can be found in Douglas, aka Jackalope City, four hours southeast of Cody. This roadside attraction is worth a stop on a drive through the Equality State.

Old Trail Town, a seasonal outdoor museum showing authentic 1890s frontier buildings, contains thousands of artifacts from the Old West.

country and have earned Cody the nickname Rodeo Capital of the World. Competitors take on challenges like riding bucking broncos, bull riding, barrel racing, and team roping. It's a thrilling spectacle that captures the spirit of the West.

There's no shortage of adventure outside town, too. Stop by Old Trail Town, a collection of restored historic buildings in a museum that depicts the frontier West. Continue to Buffalo Bill Reservoir, created by the Buffalo Bill Dam of the Shoshone Project in 1910, one of the first high concrete dams built in the United States. Today, the reservoir offers fishing, boating, camping, and hunting in the summer.

To fully experience Cody, stay in a log cabin at one of many guest ranches in town. The late afternoon sun stretches along the windswept sagebrush-filled plains, where wild mustangs still roam free, and visitors may spot a bald or golden eagle soaring across the mountain peaks.

TALK LIKE A LOCAL

"MEALTIME"

For Wyomingites, dinner is lunch, and supper is dinner, which might throw off out-of-towners. In the 19th century, dinner (lunch) was the biggest meal of the day to properly fuel farmers and ranchers working long hours. Supper was a lighter meal savored after all the chores were complete. In Wyoming, "dinner" still refers to the main meal, usually eaten around midday.

DESTINATIONS BY LOCATION

ACKNOWLEDGMENTS

Getting the opportunity to explore what felt like all the nooks and crannies of the United States profoundly changed the way I view the world, in the best way. I'll be forever grateful for this experience, which was truly one of the coolest things I've ever done.

To all the community leaders, small business owners, and small-town residents who welcomed me with open arms and enthusiastically shared their passion for the places they live, thank you. I loved seeing the world through your lenses. To all the friends, family members, and colleagues who shared their experiences and memories about small towns I did not get to visit in person, thank you. My research came to life through your stories.

To my wonderful agent, Kristina Sutton Lennon, thank you for encouraging me to find my next idea and for your unwavering support throughout the years.

To National Geographic and my editor, Allyson Johnson, thank you for your excitement, kindness, and collaboration throughout the research, travel, and writing process. And to the entire team behind the pages—associate editor Tyler Daswick, art director Nicole Miller Roberts, senior photo editor Meredith Wilcox, senior production editor Michael O'Connor, and many others—I'm so proud of the beautiful book we created together.

To my incredible mom, Lori, for acting as my unofficial travel agent and for joining me on so many of these small-town adventures, I truly could not have done it without you. To my dad, Mark, for always inspiring me to dream big and work hard to turn my passions into realities. To the friends and family who met me along the way—Katie in Hood River; Caroline in Highlands; Fran, Jay, and Kasey in La Conner. And to my loving husband and partner-in-adventure, Humberto, for the love, patience, and support you show me every day, but especially while writing this book. Thank you a million times over.

ILLUSTRATIONS CREDITS

Cover, Backyard Productions/Alamy Stock Photo; back cover, Chuck Haney/DanitaDelimont/Alamy Stock Photo; 2–3, Leah Nash/National Geographic Image Collection; 4–5, Sean Pavone/Shutterstock; 6, Danita Delimont/Adobe Stock; 8–9, Patrick Frilet/hemis/Alamy Stock Photo; 10, David S. Miller; 12–3, Albert Pego/iStock/Getty Images; 14, Beth Dixson/Alamy Stock Photo; 16, Jeff Goldberg/Esto/Redux; 18–9, Tony Cenicola/The New York Times/Redux; 20, Greg Dale/National Geographic Image Collection; 22–3, Walter Bibikow/awl-images; 24, Greg A. Hartford; 26–7, James Talalay/Alamy Stock Photo; 28 (UP), Harry Collins Photography/Shutterstock; 28 (LO), StockFood/Andre Baranowski; 28–9, Jason Busa/Dreamstime; 30, Benjamin Williamson; 32, Matthew Rakola; 34–5, Good Boy Manufacturing; 36 (BOTH), Matthew Rakola; 36–7, Scenic Corner/Shutterstock; 38, Jon Bilous/Alamy Stock Photo; 40, Edwin Remsberg/Alamy Stock Photo; 42–7, Alison Shaw; 48, Achim Multhaupt/laif/Redux; 50, Mauro Toccaceli/Alamy Stock Photo; 52, Winston Tan/Shutterstock; 54–5, Imagedoc/Alamy Stock Photo; 56, Sean Pavone/Dreamstime; 58–9, Randy Duchaine/Alamy Stock Photo; 60 (UP), Brian Skerry/National Geographic Image Collection; 60 (LO), Norman Eggert/Alamy Stock Photo; 60–1, courtesy Peter Mead, Loaded Question Brewing Co.; 62, John Van Decker/Alamy Stock Photo; 64–5, EQRoy/Shutterstock; 66 (UP), David Trozzo/Alamy Stock Photo; 66 (LO), William Thomas Cain/Alamy Stock Photo; 66–7, madeleine.elizabeth/Shutterstock; 68, Walter Bibikow/DanitaDelimont/Alamy Stock Photo; 70, art: Richard Serra, "Torqued Ellipses" from Dia: Beacon in Beacon, NY/© 2025 Estate of Richard Serra/Artists Rights Society (ARS), New York; photo: dpa/Alamy Stock Photo; 72–3, Ivan Kokoulin/Dreamstime; 74, David A. Reese; 76–7, Jonathan Cohen/Alamy Stock Photo; 78, Allen Brown/Alamy Stock Photo; 80, Joe Geronimo; 82–5, Samantha Decker; 86 (UP), Amy Toensing/National Geographic Image Collection; 86 (LO), Walter Bibikow/DanitaDelimont/Alamy Stock Photo; 86–7, Michael Ventura/Alamy Stock Photo; 88, Blair Seitz; 90, cmart7327/iStock/Getty Images; 92, Justin Cash; 94–5, Lake Champlain Chocolates; 96 (UP), Mira/John Greim/Alamy Stock Photo; 96 (LO), Paul O. Boisvert/The New York Times/Redux; 96–7, kjarrett via Flickr (CC by 2.0); 98, Brian Jannsen/Alamy Stock Photo; 100–1, Peter Frank Edwards/Redux; 102, Grand Hotel Golf Resort & Spa; 104, Pat & Chuck Blackley/Alamy Stock Photo; 106–7, ReTreet, LLC; 108, Amanda via Flickr (CC by 2.0); 110–1, Beth Hall/The New York Times/Redux; 112 (UP), Stephen Saks Photography/Alamy Stock Photo; 112 (LO), Arkansas

Department of Parks, Heritage and Tourism; 112–3, Wirestock Creators/Shutterstock; 114, Sean Pavone/Alamy Stock Photo; 116–7 and 118 (UP), N.V. Deremer—Deremer Studios, LLC; 118 (LO), moonbeampublishing/Hal and Kirsten Snyder; 118-9, N.V. Deremer—Deremer Studios, LLC; 120, CreativeStudio79/Shutterstock; 122, James Quine/Alamy Stock Photo; 124–5, Gianfranco Vivi/Shutterstock; 126, Randall Hyman; 128–9, Ian Dagnall/Alamy Stock Photo; 130, Sally Weigand/Alamy Stock Photo; 132–3, ©2019 Bernheim Forest and Arboretum. All rights reserved. "Little Nis" figure created by Thomas Dambo. Photo by Trey Thomas/Shutterstock; 134, Pat & Chuck Blackley/Alamy Stock Photo; 136, Paducah Convention & Visitors Bureau; 138–9 and 140 (UP), Bob Bell/Driving Backroads; 140 (LO), Paducah Convention & Visitors Bureau; 140–1, domonabikeUSA/Alamy Stock Photo; 142, @cedricangeles; 144, Mathew Risley/Shutterstock; 146–7, Tim Mueller Photography; 148–151, Visit Natchez; 152, Walter Inglis Anderson (1903–1965)/East Wall, The Little Room Murals, c. 1953/House Paint on Paneling/Gift of the Family of Walter Anderson/Walter Anderson Museum of Art, Permanent Collection; 154, John Wollwerth/Alamy Stock Photo; 156–7, Peter Noebels/Alamy Stock Photo; 158, Bilanol/Shutterstock; 160–1, Tim Lenz/OTTO; 162 (UP), Allen Creative/Steve Allen/Alamy Stock Photo; 162 (LO), Peter Frank Edwards/Redux; 162–3, Robbie George/National Geographic Image Collection; 164, Lisa S. Engelbrecht/DanitaDelimont/Alamy Stock Photo; 166–7, Joanne Dale/Shutterstock; 168 (UP), Zoonar/Alex Grichenko/Alamy Stock Photo; 168 (LO), Castle Light Images/Alamy Stock Photo; 168–170, Peter Frank Edwards/Redux; 172, Jay Huron—caseSensitive Photos; 174–5, jmsilva/iStock/Getty Images; 176, Carol Guzy/The Washington Post via Getty Images; 178–9, Jeffrey Isaac Greenberg/Alamy Stock Photo; 180, Zack Frank/Shutterstock; 182–3, Sean Pavone/iStock/Getty Images; 184, Mark Summerfield/Alamy Stock Photo; 186–7, Inge Johnsson/Alamy Stock Photo; 188, Nick Fox/Shutterstock; 190–1, Gary A. Clendening; 192, Greg Disch; 194, Brian Snyder/Reuters/Redux; 196–7, Karl Johaentges/robertharding; 198 (BOTH), Michael DeYoung/TandemStock; 198–9, Ben Keough; 200, Inge Johnsson/Alamy Stock Photo; 202, Bonnie Ann Cain-Wood via Flickr (CC By 2.0); 204, Alexandra Buxbaum/Alamy Stock Photo; 206–7, SK Miller/Alamy Stock Photo; 208 (UP), RFStock/Alamy Stock Photo; 208 (LO), Justin Tipton; 208–9, George Ostertag/Alamy Stock Photo; 210, Skipper Plitt; 212, Tosh Brown/Alamy Stock Photo; 214–5, Witold Skrypczak/Alamy Stock Photo; 216, Mackenzie Smith; 218, Michael Hanson/Cavan Images; 220–1, Fotoluminate LLC/Shutterstock; 222–3, Mark Edward Dawson/@nomadicfrog; 224, Danita Delimont/Shutterstock; 226–7, David S. Swierczek/Shutterstock; 228 (UP), Randy von Liski/Flickr; 228 (LO), Ulysses Suites; 228–9, Galena Cellars Vineyard & Winery; 230, Bruce Leighty/Alamy Stock Photo; 232, Alexey Stiop/Shutterstock; 234, Steve Heap/Shutterstock; 236, Neal Johnson/Shutterstock; 238–9, yosmoes815/Shutterstock; 240, Jim Richardson; 242, Gerard + Belevender; 244–5, Wildnerdpix/Shutterstock; 246 (UP), Jennifer McCallum/Alamy Stock Photo; 246 (LO), Michael Deemer/Shutterstock; 246–7, Jeffrey Isaac Greenberg/Alamy Stock Photo; 248, Susan B Sheldon/Shutterstock; 250–1, Gary Jesswein; 252, Timothy

Mulholland/Alamy Stock Photo; 254, Jim Gehrz/Minneapolis Star Tribune/ZUMAPRESS/Alamy Stock Photo; 256-7, Brandon Bartoszek; 258 (UP), "1884 Upper St. Croix Logjam" mural by Randall Raduenz, photo by Richard Ebert, Encircle Photos; 258 (LO), CNMages/Alamy Stock Photo; 258-9, WireStock/Alamy Stock Photo; 260, Jumping Rocks/Universal Images Group via Getty Images; 262, WireStock/Alamy Stock Photo; 264-5, Rachael Martin/Shutterstock; 266, Jenn Ackerman and Tim Gruber; 268-9, Arbor Day Farm; 270, Chuck Haney; 272, Viktor Posnov/Alamy Stock Photo; 274-5, JustAJar Design Press; 276 (BOTH), B. Wunderlich—Marietta CVB; 276-7, Mark A. Shephard; 278, Doris Bowling; 280-1, arthurgphotography/Shutterstock; 282, Cecilia Colussi/Alamy Stock Photo; 284-5, Jess Kraft/Shutterstock; 286, James Meyer/Shutterstock; 288, John D. Ivanko/Alamy Stock Photo; 290-1, Hank Erdmann; 292 (UP), Don Smetzer/Alamy Stock Photo; 292 (LO), MacReady Artisan Bread; 292-3, Reneé Schwaller; 294, Clint Farlinger/Alamy Stock Photo; 296-7, Richard Ellis/Alamy Stock Photo; 298-9, Bob Pool/Shutterstock; 300, AlaskaPhotoGraphics/Patrick J Endres; 302-3, AP Photo/Daily Sitka Sentinel, James Poulson; 304 (UP), AlaskaPhotoGraphics/Patrick J Endres; 304 (LO), Nick Garbutt/NPL/Minden Pictures; 304-5, Ken Schulze/Shutterstock; 306, Ian Shive/TandemStock; 308, Michael Runkel/robertharding; 310, Lacey Ann Johnson/Cavan Images; 312-3, Arev Hambardzumyan/Alamy Stock Photo; 314 (UP), Manuela Durson/Alamy Stock Photo; 314 (LO), Jay Goodrich/TandemStock; 314-5, Ethel Davies/robertharding; 316, Catherine Karnow/National Geographic Image Collection; 318, James Mattil/Shutterstock; 320-1, Janice Sakata-Schultze; 322 (UP), Susan Seubert; 322 (LO), AP Photo/John Rogers; 322-3, OC Stock Photos; 324, Michael W. Harding; 326-7, David Tsay; 328, Phil Schermeister; 330-1, Sean Xu/Shutterstock; 332, Dennis Hallinan/Alamy Stock Photo; 334-7, Jacob Boomsma/Shutterstock; 338 (UP), Amigo Motor Lodge; 338 (LO), H. Mark Weidman Photography/Alamy Stock Photo; 338-9, Lisa Seaman/TandemStock; 340, Ronny Karpel/Alamy Stock Photo; 342, Katie Herrenbruck; 344-5, Patrick Orton/Cavan Images; 346, Warren LeMay; 348, Carol Barrington/Alamy Stock Photo; 350-1, Greg Vaughn/Alamy Stock Photo; 352, Craig Moore/Cavan Images; 354-5, Diana Robinson Photography; 356 (UP), Chuck Haney; 356 (LO), Craig Moore/Cavan Images; 356-7, Chuck Haney; 358, Ron Koeberer/Cavan Images; 360, Danita Delimont Stock/awl-images; 362-3, Leigh Anderson; 364 (UP), Russ Bishop/Alamy Stock Photo; 364 (LO), Nancy D. Brown; 364-5, Nancy Rose; 366, David Gibb Photography/dgibbphoto; 368, John Trax/Alamy Stock Photo; 370, Marc Piscotty; 372, Francesco Vaninetti/robertharding; 374-5, Sorrel River Ranch Resort and Spa; 376 (UP), Lisa Seaman/TandemStock; 376 (LO), John Blottman/Alamy Stock Photo; 376-7, Ron Niebrugge/Alamy Stock Photo; 378-381, Sonja Peterson Photography; 382 (UP), Edmund Lowe Photography/Shutterstock; 382 (LO), Joel Rogers; 382-3, Alex Andrea Smith Photography; 384, Danita Delimont/Shutterstock; 386-7, Michael Wheatley/Alamy Stock Photo; 388, Steve Cukrov/Shutterstock; 390-1, Brown W Cannon III/Alamy Stock Photo.

ABOUT THE AUTHOR

Brenna Darling is a writer and creative with an acting and film background. After receiving her degree from Chapman University in Orange, California, she founded the blog DIY Darling and appeared as a featured host on the show *Weekend Refresh* by Tastemade, Inc, where she also worked as a writer. Her articles have appeared in *Business Insider* and *Forbes,* and she has acted in national commercials and films. She has also collaborated with major brands like Amazon, Home Depot, and Behr. Darling currently lives in Colorado, where she loves exploring and inspiring others to live a beautifully bold life.

Since 1888, the National Geographic Society has funded more than 15,000 research, conservation, education, technology, and storytelling projects around the world. National Geographic Partners distributes a portion of the funds it receives from your purchase to National Geographic Society to support their mission to illuminate and protect the wonder of our world.

National Geographic Partners, LLC
1145 17th Street NW
Washington, DC 20036-4688 USA

Get closer to National Geographic Explorers and photographers, and connect with our global community. Join us today at nationalgeographic.org/joinus

For rights or permissions inquiries, please contact National Geographic Books Subsidiary Rights: bookrights@natgeo.com

ISBN: 978-1-4262-2389-1

The authorized representative in the EU for product safety and compliance is Disney Trading B.V., Asterweg 15S, 1031 HL, Amsterdam, The Netherlands email: DCP.DL-EU.bookscontact@disney.com

Printed in China

26/LPC/1